and from Jerusalem,
HIS WORD

and from Jerusalem, HIS WORD

Stories and Insights of Rabbi Shlomo Zalman Auerbach
zt"l

by
Hanoch Teller

New York City Publishing Company

© Copyright 1995 by Hanoch Teller, Rechov Yehoyariv 4/7,
Arzei Habira, Jerusalem 97354, Israel. hanoch@attglobal.net

All rights reserved. No part of this publication may be translated, dramatized, reproduced, stored in a retrieval system or transmitted, **in any form** or by any means, electronic, mechanical, photocopying, recording, or otherwise, without permission in writing from the publishers. Printed in Israel. The rights of the copyright holder will be strictly enforced. Edited by Marsi Tabak.

ISBN 1-881939-05-7 **Registered with the Library of Congress**

20 ^{19} 18 ^{17} 16 ^{15} 14 ^{13} 12 ^{11} 10 ^{9}

Avail yourselves of inspiring, superbly written contemporary literature by the award-winning author, lecturer and educator. Hanoch Teller's books include short stories, biographies, *parshas hashavua*, and material designed especially for young readers. The 65-minute video, *Do You Beleve in Miracles?* Is a highly-acclaimed docu-drama that is a celebration of Divine Providence and Jewish pride. Filled with heart-warming episodes, re-enacted by top performers, fully orchestrated by leading musicians and enhanced by state-of-the-art graphics and effects. *The Righteous Live On* audio cassette and CD collection is an edifying and highly memorable audio experience. Each tape is an in-depth exploration of the life and times, the challenges and achievements of individuals that had such a powerful impact upon their generation that their stories should be fundamental knowledge for every Torah-conscious Jew. Each lecture of this impressive series will enrich both adults and youth from the staunchly observant to those with nominal knowledge and religious commitment. These presentations on Rabbi Aaron Kotler, The Ponevizher Rav, Rabbi Shlomo Zalman Auerbach, Frau Sarah Schenirer and How the Mirrer Yeshivah Escaped to Shanghai, will be listened to again and again and cherished for a lifetime!

**All are available at discount prices through
www.hanochteller.com.**

Distributed by FELDHEIM PUBLISHERS
200 Airport Executive Park, Nanuet, NY 10954

In loving memory of

Joseph Berman *z"l*
יוסף דב בן יחיאל מיכאל אהרן ז"ל

A great man and a noble soul
Who inspired countless others by his
Sterling example of
Integrity and *Tzeddakah*
And devotion to his family and the Jewish people.
He is greatly missed.

DAVID and TEMIMAH BERMAN
Max, Zach, Jake and Jesse

In loving memory of

Laurie Berman *z"l*
לייביש בן יוסף דב ז"ל

A great brother and friend
A tremendously kind, caring and gentle soul.
Those who knew him testified
Laurie lived Torah and then learned Torah.
He is greatly missed.

DAVID and TEMIMAH BERMAN
Max, Zach, Jake and Jesse

In Memory of
Our Loving and Inspirational Parents and Grandparents

Philip and Lillian Cooperman *z"l*

יצחק פישל בן אברהם ז"ל
לאה בת דוד ז"ל

ת.נ.צ.ב.ה.

Also by Hanoch Teller

Once Upon a Soul
Soul Survivors
'Souled!'
The Steipler Gaon
Sunset
Courtrooms of the Mind
Above the Bottom Line
Pichifkes
The Bostoner
Bridges of Steel, Ladders of Gold
"Hey, Taxi!"
The Best of StoryLines
Give Peace a Stance
Welcome to the Real World
13 Years
A Matter of Principal
A Midrash and a Maaseh
The Mini A Midrash and a Maaseh
It's a Small Word After All
In an Unrelated Story
Builders
О ТОМ, ЧТО НА ДУШЕ
E'rase Una Vez...
ועמך כולם...
בצדק תשפט...

Do You Believe in Miracles? *Video*
The Righteous Live On *Lecture Series*
The Sound of Soul *Audio Series*

From out of Tziyon
shall come Torah
And from Jerusalem, God's Word
YESHAYAHU 2:3

Our Sages teach:
"God's Word" — that is Halachah.

הרב שלמה זלמן אויערבאך
פעיה"ק ירושלים תובב"א

ב"ה, יום ...

הנני מעיד כאן כדת של תורה שידוע לי לרבני הי"ו
הרב חנוך יוסף שטה חרד וגדול וכו'
וכל אחד הנני מעיד ויודע שהוא בתכלית ההגינות
והוא שקוע מתמיד ועוסק בהרבצת
התורה מגדולי ישראל ואורחי... ועל ופה לציון
דרכה של תורה הלוי, איש ירא... אוהב ידידות
וגם כפי הבחינות, ושמענא כסאי, עולה על אצ...
ומעיד ברבים שראוי יעה לעלות לגדול תלמידי חכמים ישכנו
מעוצר הרבים כראוי ונכון ויהי' מיקי יראת ה' קבע
וע"ז בעה"ח

שלמה זלמן אויערבאך

APPROBATION OF HAGAON HARAV
ZALMAN NEHEMIA GOLDBERG Shlita

RABBI ZALMAN NEHEMIA GOLDBERG
MEMBER OF THE JERUSALEM BETH-DIN
ROSH KOLEL "DAAT MOSHE" SADIGORA
12 A ELKANA ST. TEL. 383162
JERUSALEM

הרב זלמן נחמיה גולדברג
חבר בית הדין הרבני
ראש כולל "דעת משה" - סדיגורה
רחוב אלקנה 12 א. טל. 383162
ירושלים

ב"ה יום ו' כ"ח ניסן תש"נ

הגיעני כבוד הרב הגאון
רבי חנוך יונתן עלוי שליט"א
שחבר ליבו דברי תורה ומוסר בהלכה
לזכות עולם בפניו ומעשיו הטובים שעשה
מצאתי בזה מין המעיין הטוב והישרך לכל
וראוי להדפיס כמה ספרי המחבר לזכות
ובזה אתנת רשות והסכמה שפיר
הדפיס ספריו הנ"ל לקדם ישועת
לעבודתו הקדושה והספיקו עליו אלו השנים
ויוסיף עוד שנים רבות הפרוסי קדשו בזה
ויתן לו הסכמה על ספריו התולדות
ולכן אין ספק שהספר יהיה לתועלת לרבים בישראל
ותלמידי ישאבו
ב"ה
הכותב לכבוד התורה ולמדי המחבר

זלמן נחמיה גולדברג

APPROBATION OF HAGAON HARAV YEHOSHUA Y. NEUWIRTH Shlita

RABBI J. J. NEUWIRTH
10 Bergman St. Bayit Vegan
Jerusalem, 96467

הרב יהושע י. נויבירט
רח' ברגמן 10, בית וגן
ירושלים 96467

בס"ד כ"ה ניסן תשנ"ב

כב'
מכובדנו הרב ר' יונתן שלר שליט"א
אחדשה"ט ושלמכ"ת כיאות

אין עושין נפשות לצדיקים, דבריהם הם הם זכרונם. מוטל עלינו
ללמוד ממעשיהם של צדיקים כי שיחת חולין של תלמידי-חכמים צריכה
תלמוד, אשר על כן יפה עשה ומצא ללמד לדורות הבאים את דבריו
של מו"ר הגאון ר' שלמה זלמן אויערבך זצללה"ה.
קראתי מעט, אבל מצאתי בו כדי לברכו על יגיעתו להביא לפני ציבור
הקוראים, ואין לי אלא לברך אותו, רבים הם תלמידיו של מו"ר
זצללה"ה ובודאי יכירו לו טובה על מחשבתו הטובה.
ויהי רצון שדבריו יוסיפו תורה ויראת-שמים בקרב אחינו, וזה יהיה
שכרו מכל עמלו.
וה' הטוב יתן שיזכה להפיץ מעינותיו חוצה ולהגדיל תורה
ולהאדירה.

המברכו מכבדו ומוקירו
משרת התורה
יהושע י' נויבירט

APPROBATION OF HAGAON HARAV
YISRAEL GANS Shlita

הרב ישראל גנס
רח פנים מאירות 2
קרית מטרסדורף, ירושלים 94 423
טלפון 371782

בס"ד   כ"ד ניסן חשנ"ה

כבוד ידידנו הדגול, רב פעלים לתורה ולחסד,
מזכה הרבים, הרב חנוך יונתן טלר שליט"א

הנני להביע הערכתי והוקרתי הרבה לכח"ר עבור ספריו
הנפלאים שהו"ל לחיזוק האמונה, ואשר זכה לעורר אהבת
המקום ואהבת ישראל, ע"י כתיבת תולדותיהם והנהגותיהם
של גדולי ישראל.

והן עתה כאשר כת"ר עומד להוציא לאור ספר על אדמו"ר
מרן הגרש"ז אויערבאך זצ"ל שהנהגותיו ודרכיו המופלאים
ראויים להחקק עלי ספר, בודאי יהא זה לעילוי נשמתו
הטהורה והקדושה, ובפרט שמרן זצ"ל בעצמו נתן הסכמתו
ושיבח מעשיו על ספריו הקודמים.

ולא נותר אלא לברכו שיזכה ויפוצר מעינותיו חוצה,
וימשיך לזכות את הרבים בספריו.

APPROBATION OF HAGAON HARAV AVIGDOR NEBANZAHL Shlita

בס"ד ה' פ' קדושים תהיו, ירושלים עיה"ק תובב"א

לכבוד ידידי אהובי וחביבי וכו' הרב חנוך לוי שליט"א

אשר ממשיך ירא"ש את מקום הסלאה הגאון הצדיק שליט"א מרן בעהמח"ס יבקש תורה זצוק"ל הנערץ וידו על ידינו גם כעת. שליט"א. בכתבת"ק אשר נשלחת לאות ב' שנת אהבה אותיות אלול ה'תשע"ה במצות דקדושה אמרות מאמרותיו, להמתיק את צדרות כעווי"ל לקרב את הבריות לאבינו שבשמים והגדרת הקדושה ולהתגבר אהבת ישראל ואנו מאושר הסי"ד. וידי אמונתיך תהיה ואין הסופר החיל יוקל העבודת, יעזור לו וירבה גבולו, ושלום הקהל דצה בהבל"א.

חותם מוקיוק
בברכת
אביגדור נבנצל

Contents

Approbations	XI
Acknowledgments	XXI
Introduction	XXV

❋ **Chapter One**
A Rich Legacy 35

❋ **Chapter Two**
More Precious than Pearls 44

❋ **Chapter Three**
Charity on the High Seas 50

❋ **Chapter Four**
Feasting on Torah 61

❋ **Chapter Five**
Sweet Onions 69

❋ **Chapter Six**
Learning How to Learn 75

❋ **Chapter Seven**
A Love of Learning 89

❋ **Chapter Eight**
Untitled   104

❋ **Chapter Nine**
Keep It Simple   112

❋ **Chapter Ten**
Judgments Sweeter than Honey   123

❋ **Chapter Eleven**
Designated Driver   165

❋ **Chapter Twelve**
The Ways of the Righteous   173

❋ **Chapter Thirteen**
An Expert Opinion   187

❋ **Chapter Fourteen**
The Traits of a Tzaddik   296

❋ **Chapter Fifteen**
Stringently Lenient   223

❋ **Chapter Sixteen**
Surrogate Father   237

❋ **Chapter Seventeen**
The Sensitivity of a Sage   251

❋ **Chapter Eighteen**
Touchy Subjects   273

❋ **Chapter Nineteen**
Nothing Fancy   283

❋ **Chapter Twenty**
"Alimentary, My Dear Grandson"   292

- **Chapter Twenty-One**
Making a Point of Order   297
- **Chapter Twenty-Two**
Amazing Grace   304
- **Chapter Twenty-Three**
A Unique Life-Support System   313
- **Chapter Twenty-Four**
Outpatient   327
- **Chapter Twenty-Five**
With an Open Mind and a Warm Heart   331
- **Chapter Twenty-Six**
Who Wants to Know?   353
- **Chapter Twenty-Seven**
He Caused the Widow's Heart to Sing   361
- **Chapter Twenty-Eight**
A Time for Joy, A Time for Grief   370
- **Chapter Twenty-Nine**
A Fitting Farewell   375

Glossary   391

Acknowledgments

The Chazon Ish often said that the finest source of ethical teachings (*musar*) was the biographies of *Gedolim*. After researching and writing this book, I feel I have no difficulty grasping the profundity of that statement. Allow me, therefore, to fulfill one of the myriad lessons to be gleaned from the wondrous and inspiring life of Reb Shlomo Zalman, *zt"l*, which is, of course, to express one's appreciation and gratitude.

I humbly thank the Almighty for allowing me to bring this project to fruition, and I thank His earthly minions who assisted and expedited its production. As always, MARSI TABAK was far more than an editor; her style and ingenuity are manifest on every page of this book. Reb Yaakov Feldheim was generous enough to allow me to take advantage of his Editor-in-Chief's precious time, as well as that of his staff members, Joyce Bennet and Sarah Kern. Joyce's fresh approach and positive outlook were particularly helpful.

The artistic talent of Shmuel Kaffe is a welcome addition to this book, as is the typesetting of Rabbi Ephraim and Bat-zion Stein. Itta Rochel Russak contributed of her energy and skills to type the manuscript, and Chaim Myerson collaborated richly in its research.

It is a personal honor and a tribute to the importance of this book's subject that Harav Avigdor Nebanzahl gave graciously of his most valuable time to review the manuscript and offer insightful comments and suggestions. I extend my thanks also to Rabbi Baruch Auerbach, who was always available for me when I needed to clarify matters.

As is my custom, I would like to take this opportunity to thank the individuals who have helped me in ways unrelated to this book. I offer my sincere gratitude to the Paskesz Family and their very kind neighbors, the Liebers (and Devorah Weiss too), and Dr. and Mrs. Eli Eilenberg. Paeans of praise to Rabbis Menachem Genack, Nahum Twersky, Ushie Rubin, and

Acknowledgments / XXIII

Gil Frieman. Honorable *mentschen* to those who are: Cary Sprung, Ashley Lazerus, Refael Leib Rosenberg, and Drs. Benjy Krupka and Shimshy Fireworker. I cannot overlook the generosity of BYA's staff, most particularly: Rabbis Shlomo Teichman and Avraham Greenberg; Chanie Calko and Chana Sara Plotsker.

The best tribute I have saved for last: My dear parents have been unstinting in their support, and my *aidel* wife is, as ever, more accommodating than words can describe.

Hanoch Teller
Brooklyn, New York
17 Iyar, 5755

Introduction

OUR SAGES TEACH that there are at any given time thirty-six *tzaddikim* whose merit sustains the world. The identity of these *lamed-vavniks* ("36-ers"), as they are known colloquially, is concealed from the general public, but throughout the generations the lofty honor has been ascribed to various and sundry individuals of utmost simplicity — the humble water-carrier, a modest tinsmith, the reticent synagogue beadle — whose public personae belied their innate spirituality.

XXVI / AND FROM JERUSALEM, HIS WORD

Reb Shlomo Zalman Auerbach maintained that the *Gedolei Ha-Torah* — the great Torah luminaries — are the true hidden *tzaddikim*, the saintly, righteous human beings to whom all the peoples of the earth are indebted for their own continued existence. Without the meritorious deeds of the *Gedolim*, there would be no compensating for humanity's abundant transgressions and the Almighty would long since have done away with this fatally flawed world.

But, one may well ask, in what way are the *Gedolim* "hidden"? Are their outstanding qualities not widely known and acclaimed? It would appear that they do not quite fit the Sages' qualifications for membership in that exclusive 36-ers club.

The *Gedolim* may be likened to the stars in the heavens: from a distance they appear to be nearly contiguous, one almost abutting the next; if one ascends to the top of the tallest building or the highest mountain, the distance between them seems somewhat larger. However, from the perspective of an astronaut in a spaceship, the distance from star to star is vast, and the closer he gets to them, the more aware he becomes of the truth — that the stars are in fact light-years apart. Thus it is regarding the *Gedolim*: the closer we get to them, the more aware we become of the vastness of their intellect and greatness, so vast, Reb Shlomo Zalman explained, that whatever we mere mortals perceive is but a minuscule fraction of the whole.

The Gaon's explanation was apt, and most assuredly it may be applied to Reb Shlomo Zalman himself, for he was indeed a *tzaddik* whose saintliness and righteousness were infinite. His Torah wisdom and brilliant halachic rulings were unsurpassed and defy accurate description in the English language. All the superlatives one might amass in a tongue devoid of sanctity and impoverished of Torah idiom fail to portray the soaring genius of the Gaon. Even the term "Gaon," so casually and indiscriminately applied today, does not do justice to Reb Shlomo Zalman, the *Posek Ha-dor*, for his genius was all-encompassing; the greatness of others is as dust before Reb Shlomo Zalman's intellect and perspicacity.

In his eighty-four years, Reb Shlomo Zalman Auerbach, זצוקללה"ה, touched the lives of many — in Jerusalem, in the Land of Israel, and in every corner of the Diaspora. We can but pray that his touch transmitted a minute fragment, a molecule of his greatness, to his People. If so, with the help and blessing of the Almighty, the continuity of Torah learning is assured.

❊ ❊ ❊

Jerusalem has had in recent history two outstanding *ba'alei chesed* who were known as "fathers": "The Father of the Prisoners" and "The Father of the Wounded Soldiers." Somehow Reb Shlomo Zalman, despite his crowded schedule of learning, teaching, and bearing the responsibility for the adaptation of the Halachah in modern days, found time to also be "The Father of Widows and Orphans." Yet even this exalted title fails to convey the measure of his fatherly ways, for they extended to all of *Klal Yisrael*.

It has long been my custom to go to the *Kosel* on Friday nights for services, after which, like other worshipers, I offer Shabbos hospitality to a number of the young tourists who — regardless of their level of religious commitment or lack thereof — invariably congregate at this holy site in the evenings. Perhaps it is the Divine Presence that beckons them; perhaps they are responding to some inner voice reminding them of their heritage; perhaps the all-pervading Sabbath spirit that envelops Jerusalem draws these estranged youngsters to the ancient focal point of Jewish awareness... whatever the attraction may be for them, I do not know. What I *do* know is that to have them share our Shabbos table has always been, *baruch Hashem*, a mutually rewarding experience.

One chilly Friday night, after our family and the usual array of invited and uninvited guests had already taken their seats and were about to begin the meal, there was a knock on the door. It was a neighbor, asking if we had room for two more. I happily welcomed "Kathryn and Gordon," who looked hungry and were chilled to the bone, and although I had already recited Kiddush, I did so a second time to include the late arrivals. In truth, I was a bit unsure about their religious affiliation, but decided to give them the benefit of the doubt.

As the meal progressed, Kathryn and Gordon warmed up and removed the light windbreakers they were wearing — inadequate for outdoors on a Jerusalem night, but superfluous after a bowl of my wife's hot and savory chicken soup — to reveal the symbols of their faith which dangled from their gold necklaces. "Oops!" was the first thought that came to mind; fortunately, good manners prevented the exclamation from escaping my lips.

XXX / AND FROM JERUSALEM, HIS WORD

I later consulted Reb Shlomo Zalman about the blessing-in-vain which I had recited when I repeated the Kiddush for Kathryn and Gordon. The incident had so discombobulated me that I was unable to express my dilemma intelligibly, and our conversation proceeded something like this:

"What should I do if I made Kiddush for goyim I thought were Jews?"

"If they were Jews, what's the problem?"

"No, they were gentiles, but I *thought* they were Jews when I made the *berachah*, but then I found out they weren't Jewish, so the *berachah* was a *berachah l'vatalah*."

"But if you thought..."

And so forth. When I finally made myself clear, the Gaon rewarded me with raised eyebrows and a long, drawn-out "Oooh." My heart leaped to my throat as the magnitude of my transgression was confirmed.

"Yes," the Gaon said, "that was indeed a blessing-in-vain. I'll tell you what," he continued. "*I* will accept full responsibility for this transgression. You need worry your mind about it no longer. Worry instead about always having the proper *kavanos* (intentions) for your prayers and devotions in the future."

Like a kindly father, the Gaon had lifted my cares from my frail shoulders and I, like a child awarded a reprieve after committing an infraction of the rules, fairly danced out the door.

A great man once said that the *Gedolim* are known by that title of honor because everything they do is *gadol* — even their most mundane, commonplace, or seemingly insignificant acts reflect their greatness. In this volume I have focused primarily on that aspect of Reb Shlomo Zalman's personality, the small things he did and said that were great because it was *he*, the *Gadol Ha-dor*, who did and said them.

This book contains many of Harav Hagaon Rabbi Shlomo Zalman Auerbach's piskei halachah and sevaros — halachic rulings and opinions expressed in SPECIFIC INSTANCES. They are not intended to be extrapolated or applied to any other instances. Every instance involving a matter of halachah should be brought before a competent halachic authority for adjudication.

A Rich Legacy

SHLOMO ZALMAN AUERBACH was born on the twenty-third of Tammuz 5670 (1910) to the pious Rabbi Chaim Yehudah Leib and Tzivya Auerbach. Both his father and mother were descended from well-established, learned Jerusalem families.

Young Shlomo Zalman attended the Etz Chayim *cheder* in Jerusalem, where he became the delight of the *Rosh Yeshivah*, Reb Isser Zalman Meltzer. As a young *cheder* child he learned together with Rabbi Shalom Eisen, who later became a Rabbinical Court official for the *Beis Din Tzedek*, and this study partnership continued throughout their lifetimes. Seven years before Reb Shlomo Zalman's demise, his life-long *chevrusa* passed on.

The Jerusalem of Reb Shlomo Zalman's youth was characterized by poverty and deprivation, and the Auerbach family did not escape this fate. Food was so scarce that the youthful scholar seldom had any lunch and only occasionally would feast on a slice of stale bread and a bit of halvah for dinner. His solitary meal of the day consisted of a bowl of watery soup; hunger was his constant companion. In later years, while giving a *shiur* at Kol Torah, he noticed that a particular student was absent. The boy's study partner reported that the young man was a bit under the weather. "When I was young," Reb Shlomo Zalman remarked, "if I had closed my Gemara every time I felt slightly ill, I never would have learned at all."

On *Purim Meshulash* of 5690 (1930), Reb Shlomo Zalman wed Chaya Rivka Ruchamkin, the daughter of a well-known Jerusalem educator. The Purim date of the nuptials had been deliberately selected so as not to conflict with the yeshiva schedule of Torah study. From that day on, the Rebbetzin devoted her efforts to seeing to it that her husband would not be distracted or diverted from his learning. The couple lived in the Ruchamkins' home, where Reb Shlomo Zalman was relieved of virtually all household duties and allowed to channel all his energies — mental and physical — toward the conquest of Torah study.

Relative to the Auerbachs, the Ruchamkins were well off. In their household soup was *soup*, that is, it actually contained edible bits of poultry or meat and vegetables. Unaccustomed to such rich food, Reb Shlomo Zalman's digestive system rejected every hearty meal he consumed. His in-laws grew quite concerned over the young man's apparent ill health, but Reb Shlomo Zalman dared not explain the real reason lest he shame his own family.

As a dowry, Reb Shlomo Zalman's father-in-law provided the groom with the deed to a sizeable parcel of land in the coastal town of Bat Yam. The land was undeveloped and uncultivated, but it was worth a great deal. One day a rumor spread that the British Mandatory authorities were about to levy a property tax on all landowners, and the talk of the town revolved around what steps were necessary to avoid paying this tax. Eventually these discussions filtered even into the *beis midrash*.

Soon Reb Shlomo Zalman became aware that these worries were affecting his concentration, and he decided to act decisively to put them to an end. He traveled to Bat Yam and entered the first real estate office he encountered along the way.

There the young scholar put his property up for immediate sale. The first customer to inquire became the purchaser, buying the property for substantially less than its actual value from a seller who accepted without negotiation the price that was offered. The deal was consummated.

Reb Shlomo Zalman returned to Jerusalem a happy man, satisfied that he could now learn without interruption and distraction. What could be better? Now he could concentrate entirely on far more vital issues.

In his approbation for *Chikrei Lev*, a *sefer* written by Reb Shlomo Zalman's father, Reb Yosef Chaim Sonnenfeld (Rav of Jerusalem) referred to the young Shlomo Zalman as a "clever child." Many years later Reb Shlomo Zalman related that he always believed these words of praise had actually been words of conciliation for an unintended insult.

The incident with Reb Yosef Chaim had occurred when Reb Shlomo Zalman was eleven years old. He was walking with his father when they met Reb Yosef Chaim. The esteemed Rav turned to him and asked in Yiddish, "*Yingele, host du gefregt di fier kashes?*" — "Little boy, did you ask the Four Questions?" Young Shlomo Zalman was highly offended by the question. Here he was, a serious student who had already mastered several tractates of Gemara and knew countless *Tosafos* commentaries by heart, and yet he had been addressed as though he were a barely literate child, capable only of asking the traditional Four Questions at the Seder!

This passage of the Haggadah, customarily recited by the youngest family member, actually plays a crucial role in the Seder as it opens the door to the retelling of the story of the Exodus from Egypt. Rabbi Sonnenfeld's innocent inquiry may have been his way of asking if the youth had any younger siblings. However, at the time, the young Shlomo Zalman could not bear to look at Reb Yosef Chaim.

Thus, when he saw the reference to him in the approbation for his father's *sefer*, Reb Shlomo Zalman was convinced that it was really a form of apology.

❋ ❋ ❋

When Reb Shlomo Zalman was twenty-five years old, he published his classic work, *Me'orei Esh*, on the laws germane to the use of electricity on Shabbos and Yom Tov. The *sefer* became an overnight sensation in the Torah world, eliciting the hearty approbations of the Torah giants of that time: Rav Avraham Yitzchak Kook, Rav Isser Zalman Meltzer, Rav Abba Yaakov Hakohen Borochov. Reb Chaim Ozer Grodzinsky of Vilna was also lavish in his praise.

After the publication of *Me'orei Esh*, most of the Gaon's writings were in the form of articles published in various Torah journals. Over the years Machon Yerushalayim and other publishing houses reprinted numerous essays of his which had been articles published decades earlier, some as many as sixty years earlier. Witnesses relate that when Reb Shlomo Zalman would sit down to review his writings from so long before, to prepare them for publication, he revised virtually nothing nor did he amend the text. The mental acuity these writings reflected could not be challenged even after several additional decades of scholarly erudition.

Having dealt with the subject of electricity on Shabbos, the next area Reb Shlomo Zalman tackled was *Eruvin*. On this subject as well he wrote a monumental essay with astounding novellae and practical halachic applications. Yet this booklet did not see the light of day. Many urged Reb Shlomo Zalman to allow its publication, but he never consented.

Years ago, Reb Shlomo Zalman's son-in-law, Rabbi Yitzchak Yerucham Borodiansky, had to deliver some discourses on *Eruvin*. He asked for permission to borrow the unpublished work on the subject, and Reb Shlomo Zalman graciously assented. The moment Rabbi Borodiansky read this phenomenal piece, he realized that it was a treasure more precious than gold. The *sefer* was a masterpiece most definitely worthy of publication and widespread circulation. Together with Reb Shlomo Zalman's sons, he encouraged the Gaon to allow the book's release. But their pleas fell on deaf ears. Reb Shlomo Zalman refused, never revealing his reason.

The head of Machon Yerushalayim, Rabbi Yosef Buxbaum, started working on this case as well. A close confidant of Reb Shlomo Zalman's and a long-time student, Rabbi Buxbaum was sitting next to the Rav during Friday night services in Shaarei Chesed, just one week before Reb Shlomo Zalman's passing.

There was a scant minute between the *Kabbalas Shabbos* prayer welcoming the Sabbath Queen and the beginning of the *Maariv* service, and Rabbi Buxbaum seized the opportunity. "Rebbe," he began, I've been meaning to talk to you..."

"I know," Reb Shlomo Zalman cut him off, "...about *Eruvin*..."

The conversation ended abruptly as the *chazzan* commenced *Maariv*. That Tuesday evening, two days before Reb Shlomo Zalman was hospitalized, the Gaon's son phoned Rabbi Buxbaum to report that the "miracle of miracles" had taken place — his father had consented!

On Sunday night Rabbi Buxbaum was among the hundreds who had gathered in Shaare Zedek Hospital to pray for the health of the Rav and monitor the developments, when the sorrowful news of the Gaon's passing was announced. The very walls of the hospital seemed to reverberate from the mournful sobbing and anguished laments of the family and students.

In those last days of the Gaon's life, several avenues of spiritual assistance had been pursued. Countless Psalms and prayers were fervently recited, and Torah was studied with unparalleled intensity to earn a Divine reprieve; but the family also felt it would be propitious to work on the Gaon's writings, to demonstrate how urgently his Torah knowledge was needed by a world orphaned from its greatest spiritual luminaries. When the final annotations were made to the booklet on *Eruvin,** our generation's foremost Torah giant was summoned to the Heavenly Assembly.

There was no property in Bat Yam to bequeath to his family, no vast holdings amassed over his lifetime. Only the Gaon's Torah was left to us, his heirs and his followers, and we could not have hoped for a richer legacy.

---

* Rabbi Baruch Auerbach, Reb Shlomo Zalman's youngest son, is currently leading the team of *talmidei chachamim* devoted to bringing to light the heretofore unpublished scholarly writings on *Shas* and responsa of the Gaon. This is an endeavor which he had already commenced, at his father's behest, during the Rav's lifetime.

More Precious than Pearls

THE FINANCIAL BURDEN that Rabbi Chaim Yehudah Leib Auerbach bore was crippling. He needed to sustain his yeshiva, Shaar Ha-Shamayim, feed its pupils, and provide a monthly stipend for the married students. With the economy in Palestine at the time on the verge of collapse, and contact with the Jewish communitites abroad at its nadir, the likelihood of Reb Chaim Yehudah Leib receiving a life-giving transfusion of funds from a generous philanthropist was virtually nil.

There was no alternative for the *Rosh Yeshivah* but to borrow large sums of money, with his family's belongings as collateral. And it was surprising to no one that, with no regular injections of capital, Rabbi Auerbach was consistently unable to meet his loan commitments. The debtors liquidated his collateral to cover the outstanding loans and in due time Rabbi Auerbach's home was bereft of any valuable possessions.

The situation went from bad to worse. With nothing remaining to back additional loans, the flow of money ceased entirely and Reb Chaim Yehudah Leib's family had no other resources at their disposal. They did not even have money for food.

Reb Chaim Yehudah Leib's righteous Rebbetzin, Tzivya, could not bear to see the suffering of her children and of the starving yeshiva students. She urged her husband to offer as collateral her last remaining piece of jewelry, a beautifully crafted gold brooch, a family heirloom she had inherited from her grandmother.

This gold brooch, with a large, lustrous pearl set in its center, had been bequeathed to the first granddaughter born after the grandmother's passing who would be named after her. Accordingly, its sentimental value far surpassed its significant monetary worth. It was the only legacy the family had from this grandmother.

Out of desperation, Reb Chaim Yehudah Leib reluctantly accepted his Rebbetzin's offer and provided this pin as collateral for a loan, and the money he received sustained them all for a while. When he managed to obtain additional funds, the very first thing that Reb Chaim Yehudah Leib did was to rush out and try to redeem the pin from the debtor. But it was too late. By the time the Rabbi arrived, the pin had already been sold in lieu of repayment of the loan.

The loss of the gold and pearl brooch was a source of untold heartache in the Auerbach family. From that time on they were wont to relate with anguish in family circles that all that was left from the grandmother's pin was a hole in their heart.

The Auerbach household was now bereft of jewelry and furnishings, but the debtors did not stop coming. Up until this point the family had, somehow, managed to accept their lot with forbearance and restraint. Now, however, the debtors started removing the *sefarim* from the house, and this was too much for the family to bear.

They had witnessed the removal of their most cherished possessions and belongings with silent agony. But the *sefarim*, the holy books that were lovingly studied and pored over all hours of the day and night! These books were a part of their soul, and their wrenching cries of dismay and sorrow rent the Heavens. The family sobbed and shed bitter tears as their revered *sefarim* were carted away. One can manage in life without furniture, and even without a precious heirloom pin, but how could one manage without *sefarim*?

There is no nice way to put it: the Shaar Ha-Shamayim Yeshiva and its dean were bankrupt. Reb Chaim Yehudah Leib's financial situation had deteriorated to the point where he could not even borrow money, and he was no longer able to pay salaries or maintain his *Kollel*. As if the situation and the shame of it were not enough, a perfidious rumor began to circulate that Rabbi Auerbach, who was pleading poverty and was unable to provide the stipend for the poor *avrechim* in his *Kollel*, was in reality a man of ample means and in fact owned several flourishing orchards. One of the disgruntled rumor mongerers decided to take action and had Reb Chaim Yehudah Leib summoned to a *beis din*.

On the appointed day, Rabbi Auerbach appeared before the rabbinical court, with his Rebbetzin at his side. The head of the *beis din* looked at the two defendants standing before him with humble dignity. "Is it true that you own a numer of orchards?" he demanded.

In an instant, Tzivya responded, "Yes, honored *Rav*, I confess — it is true. We indeed have four orchards, four beautiful orchards." Her words were greeted with surprise on the part of the *rabbanim*, and glee on the part of the plaintiff. "However," she continued, "none of them has yet borne fruit. Our orchards even have names: Shlomo Zalman, Eliezer, Berel, and Dovid..."

❖ ❖ ❖

The poverty in which Reb Shlomo Zalman was raised was so acute that he would later comment sardonically to his younger brother, "You were born in the *good* times." He was referring to the fact that when Berel was growing up there was once in a long while an egg on the day's menu, one egg that would be cut in four and divided among the children.

It was not infrequent in those "good times" that Reb Shlomo Zalman left for *cheder* on an empty stomach. The only way he managed to satisfy his relentless hunger was by feasting on the words of Torah.

Due in no small measure to his undernourishment, Reb Shlomo Zalman remained physically weak for many years. His powerful emotional resources, however, more than compensated, providing him with the inner strength to overcome any and all adversity.

Charity on the High Seas

THE YEAR WAS 1931, and Reb Chaim Yehudah Leib Auerbach had embarked on what he hoped would be a profitable voyage. Like virtually all of the Jews of the old Yishuv in Palestine, Reb Chaim Yehudah Leib was in desperate need of funds. His yeshiva was in dire straits and in addition, due to his penchant for distributing charity and responding to every philanthropic plea, he was personally drowning in debt. Loath as he was

Charity on the High Seas / 51

to abandon his yeshiva, a fundraising journey to America was essential and unavoidable.

The first days of the voyage were unremarkable, and Reb Chaim Yehudah Leib passed them quietly, immersed in Torah study. But when the ship was on the high seas and at least a week from the nearest port, the marginally seaworthy vessel sprung a leak. The ocean began to pour into the hold and the ship listed as the crewmen scrambled to locate the breach in the hull.

At the captain's command, all the passengers assembled on the main deck and for the first time Reb Chaim Yehudah Leib took note of his fellow travelers. They could be neatly divided into two distinct groups: Jews of every stripe and walk of life who constituted a cross-section of Palestine of those days; and non-Jewish residents of or visitors to the Holy Land.

In times of distress, it is only natural for people to flock to spiritual leaders for guidance, and this situation was no different. All of the Jews gathered around Reb Chaim Yehudah Leib, while the gentiles gravitated to an Egyptian Coptic priest, a tall, dark-complected man in flowing black robes and a high black headpiece that bore the symbol of his religion.

The tension in the air was palpable. Reb Chaim Yehudah Leib led his followers in an emotional and highly vocal prayer for salvation, while the priest urged his followers to engage in silent contemplation. All around them the crew continued in their frantic efforts to stanch the flow of water that seeped relentlessly into the vessel. Fear spread through the crowd like a contagious disease and in no time all the passengers were infected with it. Reb Chaim Yehudah Leib could see that in order to subdue the rising panic, more drastic measures were required.

He turned to the assembled and in a voice that rose above the noise of the sea exhorted them to demonstrate their complete faith in the Almighty: "For He is a shield to those who seek refuge in Him." Having prayed loudly and fervently for hours to no apparent avail, the passengers were at a loss as to how else they might express their faith. "Behave as though you have the utmost confidence that Hashem will rescue us," Reb Chaim Yehudah Leib declared. "Simply return to your normal routine." The group obediently proceeded to the dining room to have their lunch.

By this time the non-Jews, who had found no solace for their fears in silent devotion, had drifted away from the priest and joined Reb Chaim Yehudah Leib's somewhat more vocal flock. The loud expression of prayer apparently had enabled them to vent their terrors, unlike the silence imposed by the Coptic priest. One by one, the non-Jews calmly followed the Jewish passengers to the dining room, to the amazement and profound appreciation of the ship's officers. In these desperate circumstances, they had more than enough on their hands without having to deal with panic-stricken passengers as well.

Along with their distress signals, the crew radioed word of Rabbi Auerbach's enormous contribution to the well-being of the passengers, which, they were certain, had thus far helped to avert tragedy.

While the passengers dined, neither the crew nor Reb Chaim Yehudah Leib allowed themselves a moment's respite. The search for the source of the leak went on as did Reb Chaim Yehudah Leib's fasting and supplications, both intensifying with every passing hour. When the travelers returned to the deck refreshed, they headed directly for the saintly man who had been their source of strength and fortress of courage. By this time, all those on board, save the Egyptian prelate, viewed Rabbi

Auerbach as the "navigator" who would help steer them safely to their destination.

Reb Chaim Yehudah Leib was not a "miracle worker," but he knew it was his duty to provide his followers with the fortitude to face whatever trials lay ahead. As that endless day wore on, he urged the passengers to perform acts of kindness that would merit the Lord's compassion, such as donating money to charity. They willingly complied and the collection amounted to a substantial sum. Whether as a direct result of this activity, or purely by coincidence, there immediately arose a triumphant cry from below decks as the crew at long last located the gash in the hull, and not a moment too soon.

The captain then addressed the passengers: "Thanks to your cooperation and outstanding behavior in these difficult hours, we have indeed succeeded in finding the source of the problem and repairs have already begun. Had you succumbed to panic, it is likely that we would have had to abandon ship, and who can say what terrible results that might have had. As it is, we shall be under way in a matter of hours."

✣ ✣ ✣

Charity on the High Seas / 55

Soon the ship was once again plying the seas, but for Reb Chaim Yehudah Leib, the danger had not yet passed. Now he was in possession of a large sum of money, courtesy of his fellow travelers, and this fact rendered him a defenseless target for anyone with nefarious intent. Rather than remain sequestered in the dubious safety of his cabin, he chose to linger on the deck in full view of the other passengers, and he began to devise a plan...

Sometime later, as he gazed out over the bow, a swarthy, muscle-bound ruffian approached him from behind with a club in his fist. Rabbi Auerbach spun around a fraction of a second before the blow struck. He stared into the man's eyes and uttered a holy incantation. Before the astonished witnesses, the would-be assailant was halted dead in his tracks with his arm — poised to strike — paralyzed in mid-air.

The passengers were dumbstruck at this miraculous sight. They gathered in a tight circle and observed the incredible scene. Clearly experiencing acute pain, the ruffian continued to loom over his intended victim as though frozen in a state of suspended animation. The crowd buzzed with confusion and wonder at this second "miracle" wrought by the saintly Rabbi, and then fell silent as the miracle-man himself began to speak.

"Did you intend to render me unconscious and rob me of this charity?" Rabbi Auerbach inquired of the paralyzed assailant.

The man nodded his head slowly.

"Do you solemnly promise never again to resort to violence and do you sincerely regret your actions?"

Again the man nodded, this time vigorously.

Reb Chaim Yehudah Leib then uttered another incantation and instantly the "spell" was lifted. The ruffian groaned with relief as his arm fell to his side and the club rolled harmlessly overboard.

Talk of the Rabbi's super-human powers spread through the ship from stem to stern and also caused quite a sensation in America. Passengers and crew wired ahead to report on the "wonder-rabbi" whose miracles they had been privileged to witness. Upon receiving these unusual communiques from the boat that was making its way towards New York harbor, the various organizations and authorities there arranged a huge celebration to greet the man who had managed to calm the passengers and had thereby helped prevent the loss of lives and property. City officials, representatives of the shipping line, and an honor guard of police officers lined the pier and hundreds of excited onlookers joined them.

Rabbi Auerbach, however, had no idea that the red carpet had been rolled out for him. When he saw the crowd and the uniformed patrolmen massed on the dock, the only thought that occurred to him was "Trouble!" He was certain that the Palestinian authorities had alerted the Americans to be on the lookout for a rabbi who had defaulted on many loans and was trying to escape from his debtors. True, he indeed owed a fortune back in Eretz Yisrael, but the loans he had taken had been for widows and orphans, for impoverished yeshiva students, for food and clothing and shelter for the needy. And the purpose of this trip had been to raise sufficient funds to repay those loans. But now, with his arrest imminent, Reb Chaim Yehudah Leib feared his journey had been in vain.

A cloud of despair began to envelop the Rabbi, and he quickly turned to God for solace.

In a quiet corner of the deck he recited the *Minchah* prayers, but when he completed his devotions and looked out across the harbor, he could still see the waiting throng. Resigned to meet his fate, he slowly disembarked and strode with his head high...into the welcoming arms of his well-wishers.

The crowd cheered, officials shook his hand and the honor guard paraded up and down the pier. His prayers had been answered, so to speak — he was obviously not about to be incarcerated, and the notoriety would surely go a long way in boosting his fundraising efforts.

A member of the delegation who learned from the passengers of Rabbi Auerbach's impressive oratorial skills, asked him to speak on a contemporary issue: Prohibition. Although the Volstead Act of 1919 had been in effect for some time, the inability of the government to enforce it had led many to support its repeal and the subject in 1931 was being hotly debated.

Rabbi Auerbach did not consider himself an expert on acts of Congress or the passage of laws in America, but he was eminently capable of speaking out about "the demon drink." He related that the first sailor mentioned in the Bible was Noah, the most righteous man of his time. After courageously battling the elements and succeeding in accomplishing his Divine mission, Noah succumbed to temptation: his downfall came about because of wine...

Reb Chaim Yehudah Leib Auerbach returned to Eretz Yisrael a far wealthier man than when he had departed. His son, Shlomo Zalman, listened thoughtfully as Reb Chaim Yehudah Leib regaled the family with his experiences on board the ship and all that had transpired as a result. "I understand that in order to prevent a genuine attack on yourself," the younger Auerbach said, "you paid the 'ruffian' to simulate one. After that performance no one would dare to approach you." His father smiled.

"But how could you take such a risk and urge all the passengers to give you charitable donations?" the son asked, perplexed. "If their contributions had failed to bring about salvation, they would have turned on you and called you a fraud!"

"No, my son," Rabbi Auerbach replied. "There was no risk involved whatsoever. Either the Almighty would see fit to save us, in which case the funds would go to *tzedakah*, or the ship would go down — passengers, money, 'miracle-worker,' and all."

Feasting on Torah

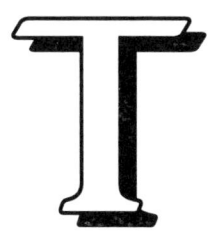ORAH was in his blood. When his family was poor, he devoured Torah in place of food. In his youth Reb Shlomo Zalman often went to bed hungry, but he took it upon himself never to go to bed hungry for Torah — never to go to bed until he had come up with some *chiddush* or new *sevara*. When he returned from prayer, he would go into his room and study for half an hour or more before coming out to eat. He said that he could never

eat until first satisfying his hunger for Torah. Reb Zalman Zalesnik, one of the *rabbanim* at the Etz Chayim Yeshiva, said that he loved to see how the young Shlomo Zalman learned with such fire and enthusiasm, that even though he was hungry, as were many in the old Yishuv, it was as though he were learning on a full stomach.

The poverty that was rampant throughout Jerusalem was keenly felt in the Auerbach home. As the eldest child, Shlomo Zalman shouldered the most responsibilities. He later commented that in light of the responsibility thrust upon him, he was technically absolved from engaging in Torah study. Yet rather than taking advantage of that dispensation, he pledged himself to adhere strictly to the times of yeshiva study delineated by the daily *sedarim* schedule. The young boy's commitment to these *sedarim* was ironclad and under no circumstance would he ever allow himself to deviate from it.

As Reb Shlomo Zalman attributed his later success to this, his commitment to his *sedarim*, he never altered it and he encouraged his students and anyone else who sought his advice to do the same. The Rav had a special room where he would learn each morning, the location of which was kept secret from the general public. He deliberately did not learn at home so that he would be able to study uninterrupted.

While learning with a *chevrusa*, if someone were to knock on the door of his room, invariably his study partner would automatically rise to answer it, but Reb Shlomo Zalman would sit his *chevrusa* right down again. "This is the time I dedicate solely to learning Torah," he would explain gently. "If someone wants me, he'll come back later, or ask someone else his question."

Reb Shlomo Zalman related that during World War II, when everyone busied themselves with finding out the latest news on the battlefront and speculating on various developments, he hardly took notice. When someone asked him why he showed no interest in such important events that would certainly affect his life, he replied, "Of course I'm interested, just like everyone else, but surely you know that what is touted as important news one day, often turns out in a day or two to be meaningless, and all the talk and speculation surrounding it turns out to be nothing more than a waste of time. It is therefore enough for me to catch up on the news every few days, and spend only a minute or two doing so. That way I can go on learning without interruption. If I spent all day, every day, speculating about the latest news, where would that leave me?"

Reb Shlomo Zalman's *hasmadah* was evident throughout his life. He never wasted a second when he could be learning Torah. The moment he finished speaking with a student, even as the next student was opening the door and approaching his desk he would resume studying the book before him. Even as a student paused between questions, Reb Shlomo Zalman would resume his consideration of the topic he was learning. But as soon as the student began to speak, he had the Rav's full attention.

Reb Shlomo Zalman had a principle of learning at least a few lines from any *sefer* he opened. The last time he came to the Yeshiva, so many students approached him with questions that when it came time for the *Minchah* prayers, he had not mananged to learn from the Gemara that was open before him. He arose to prepare himself for prayer, but then sat down again for a few minutes and learned several lines of text before closing the Gemara. But there were times when his attention was so much in demand that he had to deny himself that pleasure. On those occasions, he would cast a longing glance back at the Gemara on his desk and sigh, "Today I didn't even open it."

The corollary of Reb Shlomo Zalman's commitment to Torah was his unswerving adherence to *emmes*. For Reb Shlomo Zalman, living in accord with the truth was not merely a virtue, but the very essence of his existence, and from a tender age he waged battles to defend its precepts. When he was just bar mitzva age, he came upon some halachic literature written by contemporary scholars that challenged the rulings of earlier authorities, and he became incensed. The young boy researched the issues and then sent off brilliant defenses of the earlier authorities to their detractors. His passion for truth rendered him oblivious to the fact that he was challenging learned individuals far his senior. Yet time after time the lad managed to vindicate the opinions that were challenged, and he caused these scholars to reconsider their writings and positions.

One time, Reb Shlomo Zalman wrote up a certain matter and asked his son, Reb Shmuel, for his opinion of the way he'd written it. Reb Shmuel replied that he believed his father had devoted too much space to explaining the *ein lomar* — the approach he was rejecting. Reb Shlomo Zalman replied that this was intentional. "I want to get to the truth," he asserted. "I do not write a responsum in order to curry favor with anyone, but rather in order to clarify the truth, and I explain the other side thoroughly so that the opposing view will be understood. That way, a reader who has the time can see the opposite side as well. Perhaps this way, the truth will come to light."

❀ ❀ ❀

When Reb Shlomo Zalman was twenty-five years old, he published his classic *sefer* about the laws germane to using electricity on Shabbos and Yom Tov. The *sefer* elicited acclaim and admiration throughout the Torah world and the book was graced with approbations from the leading Torah scholars of the time. When Rav Chaim Ozer Grodzinsky of Vilna saw the masterpiece written by such a young man, he quoted, אור חדש על ציון תאיר — "A new light will shine upon Zion," accurately predicting that Reb Shlomo Zalman's Torah scholarship was destined to illuminate the entire Jewish world.

As a young man, Reb Shlomo Zalman became acquainted with the technological breakthrough for the hard of hearing later to be known as a hearing aid. He saved his every penny at the cost of great personal deprivation, in order to purchase this device for his ailing mother who was hard of hearing. And while she was benefiting from it, so was her son: he focused his learning on the halachic ramifications of a hearing aid. Was it permissible to use it on Shabbos? Does one fulfill one's obligation to hear the *Megillah*, the shofar-blowing, or the Torah reading via a hearing aid? He carefully explored these and other aspects of the new device.

The directive in this instance, as in every facet of Reb Shlomo Zalman's life, was that upon encountering something new, one was obliged to discover the Torah's perspective on it.

When a grandson returned from a trip to America where he had attended a simcha, Reb Shlomo Zalman asked him if he had visited the skyscrapers in New York City. Abashedly, the young man admitted that, like all tourists, he had. His grandfather was intrigued. "Tell me about them," he asked, his eyes glittering. "Do you know that according to some opinions two babies could be born at the same time in such a building, one on an upper floor and one on a lower floor, and their bris would not be on the same day! Because of the height of the building, the exposure to the sun is not uniform and it could halachically be evening below while still day above." It was a source of intellectual delight for the Gaon to hear a first-hand account from someone who had witnessed such a היכי תימצי — a possibility.

Sweet Onions

BOUT EIGHTY YEARS AGO the first automobile arrived in the town of Jerusalem, a small, crumbling backwater that was just beginning to awaken from millennia of slumber and recapture its former glory. The noisy, dust-caked motor car was an unbelievable attraction. Everyone came out to lay their eyes on this miraculous invention. Even the children of the Etz Chayim Yeshiva abandoned their *shtenders* to stand on the street

and gape at this incredible innovation. All of the children, that is, except one: Shlomo Zalman Auerbach. Even as a young student he realized that there were more important things in this world, and he was busily engaged in them.

Because Reb Shlomo Zalman was always particular about adhering to a fixed schedule, he was able to accomplish much more than most people. The fulcrum of his schedule was the uninterrupted time that he devoted to learning Torah. Every second earmarked for learning was sacrosanct and could not be diverted for any other purpose. Whenever he learned, his concentration was so complete that people could be standing around vying for his attention and he would never even notice them.

Rabbi Yitzchak Hakker related that he once wished to ask Reb Shlomo Zalman a question but was loath to interrupt him in the middle of learning. Thus he stood at the Gaon's side waiting for the moment when Reb Shlomo Zalman would raise his head so that he could pose his question. After fifty minutes he finally gave up and interrupted with his question.

Reb Shlomo Zalman used to deliver a two-hour *shiur* in Kol Torah. He always started his

Sweet Onions / 71

shiur precisely at 11:00 and ended at 1:00, just in time for *Minchah*. It once happened that he was involved in a life-and-death matter regarding an operation, which caused him to arrive over an hour late for his *shiur*. He plunged right into the lesson and only much later became aware of the time. He saw that the hour for the afternoon prayers with the yeshiva had passed and accordingly, the students would have to *daven* in their own *shiur* room.

Reb Shlomo Zalman stepped out to the corridor to wash his hands before services, and when he returned to the room he happened to glance toward the ceiling. There he noticed for the very first time the electric insect exterminator which had been suspended from the ceiling of that *shiur* room for years. This device emits an ominous buzzing sound every time it electrocutes an insect, and yet, although it was right above his head and made so much noise, Reb Shlomo Zalman had never noticed it before. This was the first time he had found himself in the *shiur* room in a capacity other than learning, and thus it was his first opportunity to observe his immediate surroundings.

It is related that Reb Shlomo Zalman attributed his success in learning to the fact that he was always in the *beis midrash* five minutes before the *seder* began and never left until at least five minutes after it was over.

Not only was Torah the most important aspect of his life, it was also the joy of his life. I recall many a time when in the midst of the *shiur*, someone would mention the concept of an *Acharon* with which Reb Shlomo Zalman was not familiar and the Gaon would be so overcome with pleasure that he had difficulty continuing to speak. Rumor had it that at the time of his Rebbetzin's passing, Reb Shlomo Zalman was able to emerge from the pall of his depression only by immersing himself even more deeply into Torah study with an intensity theretofore unknown.

Reb Shlomo Zalman once quipped, "For one who learns Torah, even if he only has an onion to eat, it becomes a sweet onion."

A student in the yeshiva once told Reb Shlomo Zalman that he wished to move to a kibbutz. The Rav responded that he was not opposed, "But why take only a wagon when you can bring an entire train?" The allusion was not lost on this boy. He realized that if he were to learn more, he would have more to offer — not merely his own physical presence but a whole trainload of Torah. This conductor was last sighted still loading the train as a lecturer in an Israeli yeshiva.

❈ ❈ ❈

When students in Reb Shlomo Zalman's yeshiva were confused about their future — whether they should remain in yeshiva or begin pursuing a career — they took their doubts to the *Rosh Yeshivah*. It was inevitable for these boys to emerge from their meeting with their minds made up to devote their lives to Torah study. This decision was *not* the result of a cogent argument or heartfelt plea expressed by the Gaon. Rather, the Rav's love of learning was so infectious that whoever was exposed to it was immediately smitten. No one wanted to miss out on such a joyous lifestyle. Reb Shlomo Zalman was truly the אוהב את הבריות ומקרבן לתורה — one who loves his fellow men and draws them closer to Torah.

His sensitivity and love for his fellow man were evident throughout his life. As a student at Etz Chayim, when other boys would approach him for help in understanding some difficult point, he would always smile and move over a little on the bench where he sat, saying modestly, "Come, sit down. I'm sure you understand it yourself, perhaps even better than I do. So let's go over it again together. To tell you the truth, I don't really understand it either. Let's see, Rashi explains... and the Tosafos ask... and... There, you see? You understood it all along and didn't need me after all."

Learning How to Learn

IN 1949 REB SHLOMO ZALMAN began delivering lectures at the Kol Torah Yeshiva. His very first *shiur* was attended by all of the yeshiva's *rabbanim*, to award the youthful genius the respect and honor that he deserved. Midway through the lecture Reb Yonah Martzbach, a *Rosh Yeshivah* at Kol Torah, posed a difficult question. Reb Shlomo Zalman paused for just a moment, contemplated the matter and then confessed, "I have erred," and went on to develop a second approach.

He later conceded that his blunder had been exceedingly embarrassing. Although he had three distinct replies to the question posed, he felt that the question was still stronger than his answers. In any event, he thought it might be unseemly for a young lecturer like himself to dismiss the validity of the senior Rav's query.

Rabbi Yonah Martzbach subsequently commented, "I actually knew an answer to the question that I had posed, but I wanted to see how Reb Shlomo Zalman would deal with the issue. The fact that he admitted that he had erred was, for me, the greatest *shiur* of all."

Reb Shlomo Zalman's actions at this, his very first *shiur*, reflect his uncompromising position regarding *emmes* and *shalom* that remained immutable throughout his life.

When six years prior to his passing he stopped lecturing at the Yeshiva, the Gaon stated that his decision had been based on the fact that he was becoming forgetful and his mind was not as sharp as it had been previously. Rabbi Dovid Hechsher was incredulous. "If only I suffered your problem!" he remarked with irony. "What I wouldn't give to be as forgetful as the Rav!"

Reb Shlomo Zalman was unfazed. "If I were to forget or neglect to mention a *Ketzos* or some other important commentary in my lectures, then I would be guilty of an infringement of *emmes*." Absolute truth, and the faithful transmission thereof, was his highest priority.

The Rav never accepted any money for his own personal use or that of his family. He was able to make ends meet from the salary he received from Kol Torah, which the Yeshiva linked to that of the Chief Rabbi of Jerusalem. The reason for this parity of wages was that after only a year of serving as *Rosh Yeshivah* of Kol Torah, the Gaon had been offered the position of Chief Rabbi of Jerusalem, which he turned down.

With a large family and significant expenses, Reb Shlomo Zalman had seriously considered the offer. But as soon as Kol Torah's administration got wind of this, they hurriedly consulted the Chazon Ish in Bnei Brak, hoping he would intercede. The Chazon Ish, however, was not supportive of the Yeshiva's position. He failed to see why Kol Torah should have exclusive claim to the Gaon. "What do you want from Reb Shlomo Zalman?" he asked. "The man has a large family to provide for and needs the wherewithal to marry off his children."

Kol Torah countered that at any price they *had* to keep Reb Shlomo Zalman. Once the Chazon Ish heard that the Yeshiva was willing to bid seriously for the privilege of retaining their illustrious dean, he summoned Reb Shlomo Zalman and urged him to remain at Kol Torah and reject any other offers. As to the discrepancy in salaries, the Chazon Ish assured him that the matter was about to be resolved: Kol Torah would match the wage scale of the Chief Rabbinate and Reb Shlomo Zalman would be able to enjoy the best of both worlds. "You will be a *Posek* and a *Rosh Yeshivah*," the Chazon Ish averred, and thus it was.

It is interesting to note that the discussion of Reb Shlomo Zalman's leadership should have revolved around salary when in fact he initially had no intention of filling the position of dean on a permanent basis. In the last will of Rav Yechiel Schlesinger, former *Rosh Yeshivah* of Kol Torah, Reb Shlomo Zalman was mentioned as his preferred successor. The Gaon, however, in his great humility, believed that the role was destined to be filled by one of Rav Schlesinger's sons, and in fact declared his willingness to step down the moment a Schlesinger scion was ready to take over.

❈ ❈ ❈

Many considered Reb Shlomo Zalman's lectures at the Yeshiva to be not especially difficult. It was said that they lacked the heavy sprinkling of latter-day authorities which are customarily quoted in *shiurim* for teenage students. But the truly devoted disciple, the one who would assiduously prepare all of the commentaries on the passage of Gemara under discussion, was able to appreciate what an intricate and wondrous work each of the Gaon's lessons actually were. The Rav did in fact discuss all of the *Rishonim* as well as the *Acharonim*, but their commentaries were incorporated into his explanation of the Gemara and Rashi.

Once a student approached him after a *shiur* and commented that in light of the Rav's explanation, the *ipso facto* propounded in the commentary of the *Ketzos Ha-Choshen* now made sense to him. The Gaon responded, "*Peshita*" — meaning, of course, that had been his intention all along: to elucidate the entire matter and bring the page of the Gemara to a new level of clarity, simplicity, and depth.

Although it was well within the range of his ability to do so, Reb Shlomo Zalman did not employ his position as a platform from which to exhibit and transmit his genius. Indeed, he claimed that his educational goal for his children (including, presumably, his students) was *not* that they become geniuses, but that they not be ignoramuses!

❀ ❀ ❀

Reb Shlomo Zalman tested the yeshiva students regularly, not only on Gemara but on the *Mishnah Berurah* as well. This authoritative work of the Chafetz Chayim is the definitive Halachah text, essential for understanding the Law, yet the Rav was often disappointed to discover that even the best students had insufficient knowledge of the *Mishnah Berurah*. "The students relate to the *Mishnah Berurah* as though it were a newspaper," he lamented, "something that you read only once and even then, only the headlines. But this is not as it should be. Those who learn the *Mishnah Berurah* in this fashion will never know the Halachah. The *Mishnah Berurah* must be studied intensely and with deep understanding." He once said that a student who spends six years in the yeshiva should gain a thorough knowledge of the *Mishnah Berurah,* having devoted one year to each volume.

For many years, Reb Shlomo Zalman examined the students at Kol Torah on a monthly basis. However, when he reached a certain age, he decided to stop, explaining that the testing was too demanding for him, requiring twice as much strength as delivering a lesson. Other faculty members urged him to continue, saying that owing to his exams, the students learned better all month long. After such a persuasive argument, the Rav could not refuse, but later on when he became hard of hearing, he curtailed the testing. "If I don't hear the answers," he explained, "there is no value whatsoever to the test."

The Rav would often study together in the evenings with his son as he prepared his *shiur* for the next day. Once, they learned a passage and Reb Shlomo Zalman remarked that there were two ways to explain this, one of which was the explanation generally accepted in the yeshiva world. "Yes," his son agreed, "this is the type of Torah that today's yeshiva students want to hear."

"I know," the Gaon nodded, "but I have taken it upon myself to teach others as I learn for myself and not to take into account whether this is what my listeners wish to hear."

There are different methods employed by *Rashei Yeshivah* to present their references for the *shiur klali*, the general lecture. Some prefer to provide just enough data to allow for comprehension of the sources and their background, preserving the development of the concept for the *shiur* itself. Others offer somewhat cryptic notes so that only the more scholarly among the listeners will be able to deduce the thrust of the *shiur* in advance. Still others present detailed notes and sources while disguising the novel point of the lesson, so that its delivery will contain the element of surprise.

Reb Shlomo Zalman opted for none of the above. He would enumerate and cite chapter and verse for every aspect of the lesson that he was going to elucidate. The point and thrust of the *shiur* was anything but concealed. The Rav's interest, his *sole* interest, was to develop and strengthen students in their ability to learn Torah. He never felt a need to impress anyone — not with a dazzling array of references, not with ingenious delivery, not with showmanship. The lesson itself, pure and simple, was impressive enough.

The correct methodology in studying Torah, the Rav maintained, is first to ferret out the Gemara's reasoning and then to follow that reasoning to its logical conclusion. He never tired of reminding his students of the importance of straight thinking and logic, often quoting Reb Chayim Volozhin: "The main thing is to hold on to the straight explanation (*sevara*). An explanation — even a clever one — which does not ultimately reach the goal of absolute truth should be rejected."

Straight thinking and logic are what informed the Gaon's lectures and determined which commentators he would explore on a given passage. One time, a student who was dissatisfied because Reb Shlomo Zalman had not cited the opinions of many prominent *Rashei Yeshivah*, approached the Rav after the *shiur*. "Reb Shimon says such-and-such on today's topic," he pointed out, "and tries to resolve the very problem which we were discussing."

The student hardly expected the answer he received. "I know what Reb Shimon says," the Gaon replied. "But don't tell me what Reb Shimon says; tell me how *you* think the passage should be understood." He went on to demonstrate that the student himself had not really understood Reb Shimon's opinion.

❊ ❊ ❊

One day, the Rav was manifestly disappointed that his students were not as excited as he had expected them to be over the solution he had presented for a perplexing problem. "I know what's wrong here," the Gaon reflected aloud. "The reason you are not impressed with the answer is that you have only just heard the question, and the answer was handed to you on a silver platter. Unlike me, you haven't spent a sleepless night troubled by the difficulty of working it out.

"From now on," he concluded, "I shall not respond to any thorny question on the very same day it is raised. You will all have to lose some sleep over it. Then you'll appreciate the answer."

One evening before *shiur*, I asked Reb Shlomo Zalman a question about a Rambam (in the name of Rabbi Yaakov Weinberg). Reb Shlomo Zalman was very intrigued by the question. The following week, as I was bent over, chaining the rear wheel of my motor scooter to a pole, I looked up to find the Gaon standing over me with a joyful smile of his face. Unaffected by the seemingly inappropriate circumstances, he proceeded to explain the reasoning and answer my query. His joy over resolving the problem rendered him oblivious to the somewhat unusual forum for the *Rav-talmid* exchange of views.

On occasion, in response to a question or comment from a student, Reb Shlomo Zalman revised his opinion on a point he had taught. When this occurred, he would always give credit to the young man who had "shown him the truth," declaring, "I originally thought to explain this portion thus..., but student so-and-so showed me the truth and the following way is more accurate."

Those who studied with Reb Shlomo Zalman developed the capacity to think and reason clearly. Reb Shmuel Rozovski of Yeshivas Ponevezh held students who had learned with the Gaon in particularly high regard. He always said, "The students of Reb Shlomo Zalman are *ba'alei sevara yesharah* — they have the ability to think straight."

When asked what the proper system for learning was, Reb Shlomo Zalman would answer, "I don't know what the *proper* system is; all I can tell you is how *I* learned. I would study a page of Gemara or a particular topic and then review it five or six times. I would move on from *mishnah* to *mishnah* and review each of them another five or six times more, and when I finished a *maseches*, I would immediately turn back to the first page and learn through it again five or six times." Simple, really.

❈ ❈ ❈

Rabbi Meir Schlesinger, who studied under Reb Shlomo Zalman at Kol Torah and knew him well from the neighborhood, was suffering guilt pangs. "I have learned so much from the Rav," he told Reb Shlomo Zalman (addressing him in the deferential third person), "that I am constantly quoting what I was taught. Inadvertently, I am sure that I must occasionally repeat ideas and concepts of the Rav's without awarding due credit. Can the Rav possibly forgive me?"

The Gaon responded with a smile. "If you say *my* thoughts in *your* name," he told his *talmid*, "I am gratified and happy; however, I earnestly request that you not say *your* thoughts in *my* name..."

❊ ❊ ❊

At a dinner that Kol Torah hosted to honor its American benefactors, Reb Shlomo Zalman was seated at the same table as the philanthropist and his wife. The entire yeshiva was also present to award honor to their benevolent supporters.

In the midst of the affair a student approached the Rav and asked him, "Is it not wrong for men and women to sit together?"

The next day, in the middle of the general lecture, the Gaon heatedly lashed out at this youth. "What kind of brazen, irresponsible foolishness is this?" he demanded. "For a young student to *definitely* violate the Torah prohibition of shaming his teacher in order to point out what *might* be a Rabbinic restriction!"

[Author's note: I embarrassingly confess to having committed a slightly similar faux pas. At a *Melaveh Malkah* of a certain yeshiva with which Reb Shlomo Zalman was intimately connected, I approached him at the dais to ask whether it would not be appropriate to wash and recite the *ha-motzi* blessing for the rolls which the emcee had announced needed only the *mezonos* blessing. The Rav did not respond to my question and I obtusely repeated it twice more, receiving the same lack of response.

The following night when I walked the Gaon to the *shiur*, Reb Shlomo Zalman awarded me a brief and sharp lesson in *derech eretz*!]

A Love of Learning

ECADES AGO, relatives living abroad shipped a refrigerator to the Auerbach family. At the time such an appliance was still a novelty in Palestine. Reb Shlomo Zalman immediately immersed himself in examining the halachic implications and problems associated with opening a refrigerator on Shabbos, and wrote a responsum that has become a classic on the subject.

Rav Yehudah Adass consulted Reb Shlomo Zalman about a matter of communal interest. There were two approaches to dealing with the problem at hand, and Reb Shlomo Zalman asked Rav Adass which of the two was the quicker.

Rabbi Adass was perplexed as to why the "quicker" method was necessarily the preferable one. Reb Shlomo Zalman explained his criteria in this issue: "Since both approaches are sound, the one which will allow me the time to learn one additional *Tosafos* is the method I prefer."

Reb Shlomo Zalman's clarity in Torah was once expressed by his wonderment, "I can't understand why it is that when two people speak together they understand each other, but when it comes to learning, suddenly there isn't comprehension."

Reb Shlomo Zalman's method of learning was characterized by very deep and fundamental probing of a subject, and by his never relying on a merely superficial understanding. For example: If *Chazal* issued a ruling, must one extrapolate that ruling to apply to every similar case without exception, or was the ruling applicable only to the specific instance mentioned? Sometimes, under certain conditions, there was room for leniency; at other times stringency was required, regardless of the conditions. Reb Shlomo Zalman would explore his subject thoroughly, to fully grasp *Chazal*'s intentions.

Such in-depth analysis resulted in an unparalleled familiarity with the foundations of the Gemara. All of Reb Shlomo Zalman's novel and innovative rulings were arrived at through comprehending all the applications, ramifications, and qualifications of the Gemara's example. Researching the background for one of Reb Shlomo Zalman's rulings is a supreme intellectual exercise which provides a glimpse of the Gaon's genius:

Once a shopkeeper mistakenly filled an order for sugar with salt. After the customer had finished all her cooking, she discovered that nothing she had prepared was edible.

Any *Posek* would rule that the shopkeeper would have to compensate the customer for the price discrepancy between salt (which is cheaper) and sugar. But is the shopkeeper also responsible for the customer's loss in terms of the food that had been rendered inedible as a result of the shopkeeper's error?

This precise question does not arise in the Talmud. But young Reb Shlomo Zalman, who had learned the Tractate *Bava Kamma* sixty times when he was still a child, was able to marshal his breadth of knowledge and genius of application to render a most innovative halachic ruling. (The first *mishnah* Reb Shlomo Zalman learned as a child was the opening *mishnah* of Tractate *Bava Kamma*: "There are four primary sources of damage... If an ox gores a fellow ox the owner must pay..." The young child returned home from the Etz Chayim *cheder* fascinated by what he had learned. Now, while there weren't any oxen in his neigborhood of Shaarei Chesed, there *were* roosters. As soon as Reb Shlomo Zalman's father came home, his anxious son asked him, "Is the law of one ox goring another ox also applicable to a rooster that pecks a fellow rooster?"

When Reb Chaim Yehudah Leib heard his precocious son's insightful question, he announced, "I am certain that you are destined to be a *Posek* for our people.")

A *bor*, or pit, is one of the primary sources of damage, and it is halachically defined as any man-made obstruction which can cause damage from the time that it is created. In the case of *bor ha-misgalgel*, a "traveling pit" — meaning, for example, a stone placed by someone on public property, where it caused no damage to anyone or anything, but when it was subsequently moved by either man or animal it caused damage in its new location — the obligation reverts to the individual who originally created the obstruction.

Thus Reb Shlomo Zalman suggested, based on the principle of *bor ha-misgalgel*, that the shopkeeper who substituted salt for sugar was obligated to compensate his customer for all the damage that was caused. Who but Reb Shlomo Zalman could have drawn this analogy? For Reb Shlomo Zalman everything discussed in the Talmud not only was source material for halachic decisions, but had pertinent applicability to everyday life.

❊ ❊ ❊

Years ago, when Reb Shlomo Zalman was delivering his *shiur* on Tractate *Nedarim*, he read a passage of the Gemara and then stopped abruptly when a perplexing question came to mind: The Gemara related that an oath is applicable only regarding a *d'var reshus*, a permissible matter, but cannot apply to a *d'var issur*, a forbidden matter. For example, there is no validity to an oath to abstain from eating *treif*. Likewise, an oath is not applicable to a *d'var mitzvah*: one cannot make an oath to eat matza at the Seder, for we are already sworn from the time of Mount Sinai to uphold the Torah's precepts and there is no room for personal volition.

"Thus," asked Reb Shlomo Zalman, "where indeed is there such a thing as a *d'var reshus*? If a person eats only because of his desire for tasty food, that is not a *d'var reshus* but a *d'var issur*. And if a person eats in order to have the strength to be able to learn and perform mitzvas, that is not a *d'var reshus* but rather a *d'var mitzvah*. So then, when, pray tell, is a *d'var reshus* ever applicable?"

Reb Shlomo Zalman's question, of course, was a reflection of his personal lifestyle. Every action he took and every thought he conceived revolved around doing the will of God. Thus he could not fathom the existence of a *d'var reshus*, for every action is governed by the will of God, and if it is not His will, then it is forbidden.

Many have learned this passage in the Gemara without even noticing the confounding enigma which Reb Shlomo Zalman raised.

❋ ❋ ❋

As Torah was the fulcrum of his life, his acts and thoughts were always based on the rulings in the *Shulchan Aruch* and guided by the lessons he gleaned from *Chazal* and the Torah itself:

Regarding the incident with Sarah and Avimelech the King of Gerar, the Torah records:

"Then Avimelech summoned Avraham and said to him, 'What have you done to us? How have I sinned against you that you brought upon me and my kingdom such great sin? Deeds that are not to be done you have done to me.' And Avimelech said to Avraham, 'What did you see that you did such a thing?' "

"And Avraham said, 'Because I said, "There is no fear of God in this place and they will kill me because of my wife." ' "

Reb Shlomo Zalman asked why the Torah repeats "And Avimelech *said* to Avraham" twice in the same monologue.

He answered this question with an insight which reflected his outlook and constant integrity: When Avimelech began to hurl accusations and speak heatedly to Avraham in a brazen tone, Avraham did not respond. A man of integrity would not respond to such accusations. It is forbidden to respond to a fool, who speaks foolishly.

Only when Avimelech calmed down and spoke in a manner befitting to Avraham, did Avraham *Avinu* respond.

This was the formula Reb Shlomo Zalman followed in his lifetime, always answering precisely what was asked, in a straightforward manner and with astute insight.

Another example of the extent to which Reb Shlomo Zalman adapted his life to conform with the lessons he derived from *Chazal* — above and beyond what is written in the *Shulchan Aruch* — is illustrated by his interpretation of the well-known passage in Tractate *Berachos*: "The early *Chasidim* (pious ones) would meditate and introspect for one hour before, and one hour after, prayer."

Regarding the hour prior to prayer, the Mishnah states explicitly that the purpose of this introspection was to focus one's heart upon serving God. But what, asked the Gaon, is the purpose of the hour *after* prayer? The Talmud does not elucidate.

Reb Shlomo Zalman explained that during the course of prayer one is inspired to improve himself and perfect his ways. However, during prayer itself one is forbidden to stop to re-examine his life and consider practical means to improve his ways. One may not interrupt a session with the King of all kings to engage in self-analysis.

This, then, is the purpose of the hour after prayer. This time is to be devoted to practical implementation, to translating the inspiration into the concretization of personal improvement.

In light of this observation, it was no surprise to see the intense devotion that Reb Shlomo Zalman invested in his prayers. To watch the Gaon *daven* was to witness a man standing before the King. His *Shemoneh Esreh* would last a quarter of an hour on a regular weekday and for the entire time he stood erect and perfectly still — even when he was at his weakest.

In his later years he would often return home exhausted from the intense concentration of his prayers. He recited every prayer and blessing with profound *kavanah*. A noted

Jerusalem *tzaddik* once advised: If you would like to see how to talk to God, go and watch how Reb Shlomo Zalman recites a blessing.

When Reb Shlomo Zalman would leave his house for the evening *Ma'ariv* prayers, there would sometimes be as many as twenty people waiting outside wishing to ask him quick questions as they accompanied the Gaon to services. Reb Shlomo Zalman, of course, was in a rush to get to *Ma'ariv* on time, and those who had assembled were in a rush to get a response to their pressing questions.

It was not unusual for the assembled to confuse and delay the Gaon. This was very disconcerting to Reb Shlomo Zalman, who always liked to be on time. Thus in the not-too-infrequent event that he was late, he would *daven* in the room adjacent to the shul and only actually enter when everyone was already standing for the *Shemoneh Esreh*. This way he would not trouble people to stand up in his honor.

At the end of his life, Reb Shlomo Zalman's *Shemoneh Esreh* was much longer than it had been in earlier years. When his son, Reb Shmuel, asked him why this was so, he explained, "I am older now and lack the strength to concentrate as I did before. I therefore must rest between each blessing."

He once told someone: "The best advice I can give you is to concentrate on your one hundred daily blessings so that the *baruch* is a *baruch* and the *Attah* is an *Attah*..."

Privileged was the person who saw him recite *Birkas Ha-Mazon*; this was a lesson in how the Grace after Meals ought to be recited. It was as though you heard new prayers from him when he *bentched*. His recital invested the blessings with new meaning.

Reb Shlomo Zalman would say the Grace slowly, word by word, as though each word were a gold coin he was counting. Once, the family heard him complete the *Nodeh Lecha* segment and then repeat the entire paragraph from the beginning. After he finished his recitation, they asked him why he had repeated the text. He replied that he had been thinking about something else the first time, and if, when one expresses his gratitude to God, he is not thinking about what he is saying, it is as though he has not said anything at all.

❋ ❋ ❋

Reb Shlomo Zalman loved to pray slowly, with deep concentration which allowed him to dwell upon the meaning of each word. He once confessed that it was a special treat for him to be able to *daven* in a yeshiva where the prayer service is much slower than in a regular shul where people are on a tight time schedule.

When asked why he didn't pray at the Ma'alos Ha-Torah Yeshiva in Shaarei Chesed, headed by his son, Reb Shmuel, he explained that the yeshiva was closed during intersession, which meant that at those times he would have to *daven* in the local neighborhood shul, and it would be insulting to the congregants to make them feel that they were only his second choice. Thus, despite his affinity for the yeshiva-style service, he could never take advantage of it for fear of offending others.

A newly married student at Kol Torah had a dilemma. He wanted very much to live in the neighborhood of Bayit Vegan, to be near the Yeshiva, to *daven* there, to spend his *Shabbosim* there, and so forth. His mother-in-law, however, very much wanted her daughter to live closer to her, in the Geulah neighborhood. The young man asked the Rav's son-in-law to consult the Rav on his behalf. He went to his father-in-law, and presented the situation, saying that the student wished to live in Bayit Vegan, and proceeded to give all the reasons. "He wants to continue praying in the yeshiva," he said, and at that point Reb Shlomo Zalman stopped his son-in-law.

"If he wants to pray in the Yeshiva," the Gaon asserted, "that's sufficient. He should live in Bayit Vegan." Then he added: על כן יעזוב איש את אביו ואת אמו — "'Therefore does a man leave his father and mother...' Regarding men, there needed to be a verse in the Torah to teach us this; otherwise we would not know it. Regarding women, however, there is no such verse, because it is obvious. If the student wants to *daven* in the Yeshiva, that is sufficient grounds for the couple to live in Bayit Vegan."

Rabbi Yerachmiel Fried related that once he was walking with Reb Shlomo Zalman in Shaarei Chesed during yeshiva intersession, when the Gaon asked a youth what time the *Minchah* service was. The boy innocently replied that he did not know.

Reb Shlomo Zalman was distressed by the boy's response. He again quoted the Talmudic comment about how the early *Chasidim* (pious ones) would meditate and introspect for one hour before and one hour after prayer. "Clearly," remarked the Gaon, "this boy cannot spend an hour in preparation if he doesn't know what time the prayers begin..."

Approbation for Me'orei Esh from Rav Avraham Yitzchak Kook, זצ״ל, Chief Rabbi of Israel.

הסכמת הרב הראשי שליט״א.

ב״ה יום ד' לחדש כסלו תרצ״ח

ראה ראיתי פעולת איש מהיר במלאכתו מלאכת שמים אברך כמדרשו וברוחו פי שנים הרב הגאון החריף ובקי עתיר נכסין בחונה של תורה מו״ה שלמה זלמן בן ידידנו הרב הגאון המפורסם מו״ה חיים יהודא ליב אויערבאך שליט״א שהראה חזותו לפני במחברת "מאורי אש" על עניני כבוי והבערת החשמל שהתחילו רבים וכן שלמים לעסוק בשאלה זו להזהיר לעם קדוש שלא יכשלו בהליכתם ולעשות בזה כתורה וכמצוה, והרב המחבר שליט״א האריך למעניתו ואסף וסידר מערכה יפה בפלפול וסברא ובינה יתירה להציע לפני גדולי הדור חכמי תורה מה שיש בענין זה המחודש מקרוב להחבירה, ושפיר שומעניא כי העלה והביא ספר ערוך ברב תושיה על הספר היקר "שב שמעתתא" לרבנו בעל קצוה״ח המלא אוצרות תושיה בכלל גדול ועקרי ההלכה בחזקה ורובא וספיקות וענפיהם המרובים המסתעפים למקצועות רבים בתורה, על כן אמרתי להודיע לעדת קודש יתרון כשרו ונעימת חבלו למין תחזקנה ידיו לאחוז בסנסיני תוה״ס ולעלות למעלה למעלה במעלות הקודש, ותושיה לרוב יודיע בעז״ה כיד כשרונות הטובים והמצויינים אשר חלק לו ד', וכמדת שקידתו הגדולה על דלתי התורה יהי' זה שכרי ועתרת ברכה כנה״י ונפש ידידו מברכו באה״ר מהר הקודש מירושלים.

הק' **אברהם יצחק הכהן קוק**

הרב הראשי לארץ ישראל

האב״ד בעיה״ק ירושלים תובב״א

Approbation for Me'orei Esh from Rav Isser Zalman Meltzer, זצ״ל

הסכמת מורי ורבי שליט״א

ב״ה יום ד' כ״ה לחדש אלול תרצ״ח

מע״כ אהובי חביבי הרב הגאון הנעלה מו״ה שלמה זלמן בהרב הגאון מוהרה״יל אויערבאך שיחי' מגדולי לומדי ישיבתנו עץ חיים התנוסס לתפארה עוד מימי נעוריו ובחרותו לעילוי עצום בטהרות שכלו וסברתו הישרה. ועתה אם שעודנו אברך צעיר לימים הוסיף חכמה ותבונה רבה כאחד הגדולים המפורסמים ועשה חבור מפואר על חשב שמעתתא ביאורים וחדושים נעלים ומצויינים בסברות ישרות ועמוקות, כן עתה בזמן קצר מעת שהתחילו הגדולים לדבר בשער קול תורה ע״ד ענין האלקטריא הספיק לחבר חבור רחב על כל פרטי הספיקות בזה, ובכל חלקי הספיקות הוא מבאר ומחדש חדושים עמוקים ומתוקים, ע״כ ידי תכון עמדו להו״ל את ספריו אשר המעיינים יהנו מדבריו וגם יהי' התעוררות לחכריו ובני גילו בתוה״ק ללון בעומקה של הלכה כמותו ותפוץ חכמה ותרבה הדעת, ויתן ד' שיקוים כי מציון תצא תורה וגו'

הכו״ח יום הנ״ל

נאם **איסר זלמן מלצר**

(האב״ד ור״מ סלוצק)

ר״מ ראשי לחישיבה וראש המוסד הכללי עץ חיים בעיה״ק ירושלם ת״ו

Approbation for Me'orei Esh from Rav Abba Yaakov Hakohen Borochov, זצ״ל

הסכמת בעל "חבל יעקב" שליט״א

ב״ה

הנה כאשר היה למראה עיני איזה עלים נדפסים מהספר "מאורי אש" על עניני כבוי והבערת חשמל ביו״ט שהתחילו לא כבר לאסוקי בשמעתא דנא גדולי ירושלם כפי שנדפס פסקי פסקי בשער קול תורה ועתה שמצאתי בהעלים הנדפסים הללו אחרי שמתי עיוני בהם שפר והתעורר אברך כמדרשו רך בשנים ואב בחכמה ומרחיב בהלכה זו בכל פרטי הספיקות עפ״י יסודות נאמנים מש״ס ופוסקים ראשונים ואחרונים בעומק העיון ובהגיון ישר הוא ניהו האברך הרב הגאון המחודד בעומקי של הלכה כש״ת מו״ה שלמה זלמן שליט״א בהרב הגאון המפורסם מו״ה חיים יהודא ליב אויערבאך שליט״א בעמח״ס חכם לב. מצאתי חובה בנפשי להודיע בשער בת רבים שהספר הלזה יהי' כ״כ נרחב להמעיינים בזה לאסוקי שמעתתא דנא אליבא דהלכתא שלבד שהוא מעורר ומאיר הרבה בענינים המסתעפים בזה להלכה דנא ממקורות נאמנים־הוא מזהיר הפרטים בתהלוכות הארת החשמל הנוגעים להבעיינים בדינא הלזה שלא כל גדולי תורה בקיאים בפרטי תהלוכות הארת החשמל לכן מצוה גדולה לחזקו ולסעדו שיפוצו מעינותיו חוצה יגדיל תורה ויאדיר.

כה־דברי המדבר למען כבוד התורה יום ה' ח' לח' כסלו תרצ״ח ירושלם עיה״ק

נאם **אבא יעקב הכהן ברוכוב**

בעה״מ שו״ת "חבל יעקב"

לפנים רב ואב״ד דק״ק וואלקאוויסק וכעת מתושבי ירושלים.

Untitled

THERE WAS NO DOUBT in the mind of any of the guests at the bris that Reb Shlomo Zalman would be the *sandek*. As the most prominent personage present, it was only fitting that he receive the highest honor. The youthful father of the newborn, in an effort to distribute the various honors in an orderly fashion, had prepared a detailed list which he relayed to the *mohel*, who was to call out the names of the honorees and their assigned tasks as the ceremony proceeded.

Among the guests at this affair was Reb Shlomo Zalman's nephew, whose name is also Shlomo Zalman Auerbach, a bright young man with a promising future ahead of him. The new father intended to honor this friend with "*chaika shelishis*" — not a particularly lofty assignment, akin in status to the honor of handing the pen to a witness who signs a wedding contract. But when the number of honorees at a bris exceeds the number of genuine honors available for distribution, provision is made to include as many as possible in the ceremony.

When the *mohel* called out the name "Reb Shlomo Zalman Auerbach," however, it was not the young nephew who rushed forward to receive this bargain-basement honor, but his illustrious namesake. It never occurred to the humble *Gadol* that the highest honor, that of *sandek*, was being reserved for *Maran Ha-Rav Ha-Gaon*, Reb Shlomo Zalman Auerbach.

When asked by a *New York Times* reporter how he had gotten to be *Gadol Ha-dor* (a question that could only come from a gentile journalist), Rabbi Moshe Feinstein, replied: "Well, it begins with one person asking a question and receiving an answer he can live with, which is yet in perfect consonance with Halachah. He tells his friends, I suppose, and they too bring their questions and they too receive viable, halachically sound answers. And so it goes. In time, one becomes accepted."

Reb Moshe's humility was legendary. The humility of Reb Shlomo Zalman, it seems, was state-of-the-art. On the eve of his passing, the sad event was routinely announced in the Israeli media. But it was only hours later, after the radio and television stations were inundated with phone calls and faxes from all over the world, that the authorities became aware of the magnitude of the event. Only then did the Jerusalem police force begin to prepare for a funeral of unprecedented proportion, a procession which would bring the capital to a standstill and shut down the main arteries of the Jerusalem metropolitan area for the whole day.

The authorities were at a loss to comprehend. "How can it be that this rabbi was so important," they asked openly, "and we never heard of him?!"

Perhaps it is a sign of greatness in the Torah world, wherein our foremost leaders are not democratically elected by a show of hands or a secret ballot, but are universally acknowledged and recognized by Torah Jewry as the ultimate halachic authorities. They need not make headlines or public appearances to gain our undivided attention. On the contrary; the most illustrious *Gedolim* are often the most reticent, shunning the limelight in favor of the *beis midrash*.

Reb Shlomo Zalman Auerbach was the undisputed *Rashkebehag* — *Rabban Shel Kol B'nei Ha-golah*, that is, the leader of world Jewry. And yet, when he received a letter with this honorific appended to his name he became so incensed that he refused to even open the envelope. He deplored the numerous titles with which people addressed him or referred to him and did not hesitate to express his low opinion of the popular practice. When a local religious newspaper referred to him as *Posek Ha-dor*, he dashed off a furious letter to the publisher threatening to cancel his subscription if the offense were ever repeated!

Reb Shlomo Zalman believed that the titles of honor that were bestowed upon him were unnecessary and he even considered some untrue. When his son Reb Baruch wrote a *sefer* and referred to his father as *Maran*, Reb

Shlomo Zalman was irate. "You're my own son," he exclaimed, "and look what you are doing to me. If you do not take this term out of your *sefer*, I shall remove my letter of approbation!"

Someone once brought a *sefer* he had written to Reb Shlomo Zalman's house. When the Gaon opened it up he saw that the author had inscribed it with extremely lavish and, to his mind, bombastic and pompous honorifics. As soon as the man departed, Reb Shlomo Zalman ripped out the page with the grandiose titles, and only then did he place the volume in his bookcase alongside his other *sifrei kodesh*.

Reb Shlomo Zalman's nephew once wrote him a letter asking him four halachic questions. The Rav responded to each of the queries, and then closed with these words: "It is 'very not nice' of you to write all these titles to me, especially on the envelope."

The nephew later asked his uncle to explain what he meant by "very not nice." "Is there a difference between 'not nice' and 'very not nice'?" he inquired.

Reb Shlomo Zalman explained himself. "Do you think it matters or interests the mailman if I am a Rav or a Gaon, or the other exaggerations you wrote? The poor man sweats in the summer, gets drenched in the winter, and, if that isn't enough, you have to complicate his job by making him struggle with all these acronyms and fancy titles to decipher whom the letter is for. It is inexcusable *gezel zeman*, the robbery of someone's time, and לא תרדה בו בפרך. It is strictly forbidden to write all of this on the envelope. All that is necessary and all that should be written is the name. Period."

In his later years, when it became difficult for Reb Shlomo Zalman to read, he would ask his devoted disciple Reb Avigdor Nebanzahl to read his letters for him aloud, insisting that Rav Nebanzahl read only the body of the letter and skip any praise or titles. This remark prompted Rav Nebanzahl to relate to his Rebbe the story of how Rabbi Akiva Eiger once received a letter from a simple Jew, addressed to *Ha-Rav Ha-Gaon Rashkebehag*, and Rabbi Akiva Eiger responded to the letter-writer addressing him with the very same title. When this unsophisticated fellow eventually met Rabbi Akiva Eiger, he complained that he was *not* a Gaon, and certainly not the leader of world Jewry! Rabbi Akiva Eiger innocently replied, "I saw that this is what people write in letters to me, so I assumed it must be the customary form of address in every letter."

Reb Shlomo Zalman told his beloved student that the story could not be genuine and must have its source in the so-called Enlightenment, which sought to ridicule Rabbi Akiva Eiger.

"There is no doubt," the Gaon asserted, "that Rabbi Akiva Eiger knew *precisely* who he was and that he was indeed the *Rashkebehag*; he clearly would not have written such a title to every person with whom he corresponded."

Hearing his teacher's words enabled Rav Avigdor to draw the same conclusion about Reb Shlomo Zalman. The Rav was indisputably the halachic authority of the generation, and the leader of world Jewry, but nonetheless he could not endure having these titles applied to him or written about him because of his enormous humility and his desire to flee from honor. In addition, he may have felt that the title *Posek Ha-dor* belonged to his *mechutan*, Rav Yosef Shalom Elyashiv.

In his capacity as *Rosh Yeshivah* of the Kol Torah Yeshiva in Bayit Vegan, Reb Shlomo Zalman invited the great Gaon who lived in that same neighborhood, *Dayan* Yechezkel Abramsky, to deliver *shiurim* at the Yeshiva. Reb Shlomo Zalman personally attended these lectures and always listened attentively.

Once, as Reb Shlomo Zalman was delivering a general *shiur* to the entire Yeshiva, Rabbi Abramsky walked into the *beis midrash*. Reb Shlomo Zalman stopped in mid-sentence and pleaded with Rabbi Abramsky to take over for him.

Rabbi Abramsky, however, wouldn't hear of it, yet Reb Shlomo Zalman continued to plead with him to deliver the major *shiur* in his own Yeshiva. Finally, Rabbi Abramsky *ordered* Reb Shlomo Zalman to continue the *shiur*, at which point Reb Shlomo Zalman relented, citing the halachic principle אין מסרבין לגדול — one may not refuse a great man.

Keep It Simple

I F THERE IS ONE WORD that typified Reb Shlomo Zalman Auerbach it is "simplicity." The simple solution to a dilemma; the uncomplicated, straightforward answer to a question; the unaffected, modest lifestyle; the direct, unadorned mode of speech — this was his way.

Countless times, his answer to questions I posed regarding either *segulos* or ambitious programs I considered adopting was simply:

תמים תהיה עם ד' אלוקיך — "You must remain totally simple to God your Lord."

Many years ago, when Reb Shlomo Zalman's father was on his deathbed, some students were quickly summoned to help complete a *minyan* so that the appropriate verses could be recited before Reb Chaim Yehudah Leib's soul departed. The assembled prayed with fervor, and when they reached the words of *Shema Yisrael*, a loud mournful lamenting emanated from the adjacent room where the women of the family had gathered. Reb Shlomo Zalman, at this most difficult hour, interrupted his devotions. He stepped into the women's room and silenced the mourners with this straightforward statement: "We are Jews and Jews do not weep this way."

Whoever had the privilege of meeting Reb Shlomo Zalman, even briefly, was taken by his pleasant nature and warmth. According to the Gaon's own admission, however, this was not his innate nature but the result of a concerted effort on self-improvement.

The Gaon told Reb Meir Goldwicht when he brought his bride-to-be to meet Reb Shlomo

Zalman, that when he was young he had been quick to anger. He was easily irritated and had very little patience. "Therefore," the Gaon explained, "I informed my fianceé as soon as we became engaged that I wished to establish a simple method whereby I would never come to anger. She agreed to give me her full support, whatever that method should be. Then in the *cheder yichud*, when we were alone for the first time after the *chuppah*, I told her," the Gaon concluded with a twinkle in his eye, "that if we were ever to disagree about anything — she is right!"

After his wedding Reb Shlomo Zalman moved into his father-in-law's house, but he would never sit at the head of the table — even after Rabbi Ruchamkin's passing. He maintained that the seat at the head of the table was reserved for the person who led the family. He was referring to his elderly mother-in-law who, because of her advanced years, was not even able to take her meals with the family in the dining room. Thus that seat of honor remained empty.

Reb Shlomo Zalman got along famously with his mother-in-law, in whose home he lived for close to sixty years. Towards the end of her life her eyesight failed, preventing her from engaging in a favorite daily pastime: reciting chapters of *Tehillim*. Reb Shlomo Zalman, ever one to harnass technology for the purpose of a mitzva, and his family for the performance thereof, simply taped — with their help — the entire Book of Psalms on a cassette so that Rebbetzin Ruchamkin would not have to abandon her life-long custom.

❀ ❀ ❀

What guided Reb Shlomo Zalman absoutely was Torah, and what was written in the *Shulchan Aruch*; one does what he has to do, not what he wants to do. Torah is reality; Torah is strength. This simple credo was demonstrated most clearly during his last two years, as his physical strength ebbed. He repeatedly chastised himself for his weakness in those final years, and as he did in his youth, he strove to overcome it. Despite the hardship, when he saw the need to do something, he would summon resources and draw his strength — no one knew from where. If a sick person needed visiting, if a mourner needed comfort, Reb Shlomo Zalman went.

Around this time, a member of the family fell ill. Reb Shlomo Zalman of course was determined to visit him. The only problem was that the patient lived in an apartment on the fifth floor of a building with no elevator, and at the age of eighty-four the Rav had great difficulty climbing steps. The impediment was quickly overcome as Reb Shlomo Zalman nominated two escorts to assist him. All in all, the Gaon made the ascent three times, with his youthful escorts puffing and panting at his side...and then a fourth time, when he went to pay a condolence call.

Reb Shlomo Zalman loved people, and most of all he loved making people happy. Smiles are often contagious — and perhaps that is why he always wore one. Rabbi Avraham Yosef Laizerzon, who possesses the largest collection of snapshots of the Gaon, noticed that there is a smile adorning Reb Shlomo Zalman's face in virtually every picture, *except* the ones in which he is holding a Torah scroll, reflecting his awe of the holy text. Not long before he passed away, the Rav gave this blessing to a young family member: "Learn well. Eat well. Sleep well. And always smile."

There was a little boy in Shaarei Chesed who used to follow Reb Shlomo Zalman around.

Wherever he went, whenever he turned around, this youngster's sweet face was there, looking up at him. One day the boy's father asked the Gaon to give the child a *berachah*.

The father had imagined that the Rav's blessing would be that the boy become a towering scholar and teacher among the Jewish people. At the very least, he expected the *berachah* which Reb Shlomo Zalman had given to the son of a prominent educator: "May your father always have *nachas* from you." The educator had not been disappointed. He felt that his son had received the blessing a loving parent would give.

The father of the little boy from Shaarei Chesed, however, was in for a surprise. For this angelic child who quite literally followed in his footsteps, the Gaon's blessing was, "Teach him to smile."

Actually, Reb Shlomo Zalman considered himself unworthy to dispense blessings, but people so frequently asked him for a *berachah* that he felt obliged to accommodate them. Basing himself on the Netziv, on the comment of *Chazal*: "Do not take lightly the blessings of an ordinary layman" — which in fact refers to a gentile, he believed his own humble blessing might have *some* worth.

Reb Shlomo Zalman had a special place in his heart for children and young people. Any child who came to his house would leave with a candy or some other sweet. The Rav once said that he would not consider it beneath his dignity to be the traditional "candy man" in shul.

A distant American relative of the Gaon's came to Israel to learn. The young boy was a diligent student, but innocent about the way of the world. When he started to date, a girl he was introduced to asked him to whom she might turn to inquire about him. Without any hesitation he recommended that she consult Rabbi Auerbach. And she did.

The match apparently was decidedly appropriate, as she was endowed with an equal amount of innocent naiveté. She went directly to the Gaon's house and told him that she wished to discuss a boy she was dating.

Reb Shlomo Zalman made himself available to answer any and all of her questions. *One hour* later, as his interview neared its conclusion, he gave her his unlisted phone number and told her that if she had any further questions she shouldn't hesitate to call. The young lady happily took him up on his offer and indeed phoned him — not once, but many times!

❊ ❊ ❊

When Reb Shlomo Zalman arose from *shivah* after the passing of his Rebbetzin, the Rav's close disciple, Reb Avigdor Nebenzahl, arrived for their usual learning session. Before beginning, Reb Shlomo Zalman commented wistfully, "There is an expression, 'What the mind cannot do, time will.' Far better," the Gaon added, "that the mind should simply *do* it."

❊ ❊ ❊

Reb Shlomo Zalman encouraged everyone, especially family members, to be "normal" and to mingle with other people. He deplored a hermit-like existence and any affectations of being removed from or above society. He instructed one of his grandsons to make a point of regularly visiting his married siblings every three weeks, a schedule which would not interfere inordinately with his yeshiva studies but which would guarantee that he interacted with the "outside world" and maintained strong, healthy family connections.

The Rav once asked a grandson if he knew how to repair a broken tape recorder. It was important to Reb Shlomo Zalman that the answer be positive: he utilized this as a measure of the boy's grasp of mundane matters, which he felt was an important aspect of his development. Torah study of course was foremost, but Reb Shlomo Zalman could not tolerate someone who was totally withdrawn from the world. He himself exhibited a healthy interest in mundane, everyday matters.

The Gaon was once walking along the street when a construction sight captured his attention. He stopped to watch the heavy machinery at work. Those accompanying him believed he was admiring the wonders of Creation, but in truth he was fascinated by the operation, as any normal human being might be.

The concerned parents of a retarded child once came to Reb Shlomo Zalman to consult him on the choice of an institution for their son. They were considering two alternative facilities, each one having certain advantage over the other. Reb Shlomo Zalman listened carefully to their description and then asked, "Where is the boy? What does *he* say about all this?"

The parents looked at one another in astonishment. They conceded that it had never occurred to them to discuss the matter with their son. "And frankly," the father added, "I don't see much *point* in discussing it. This is not something he can grasp."

Reb Shlomo Zalman was irate. אתם חוטאים בנפש הילד — "You are committing a sin against the soul of this child!" he cried. "You intend to evict him from his home and consign him to a strange place with a regimented atmosphere. He must be encouraged and not allowed to feel that he is being betrayed." The parents were speechless.

"Where is the boy?" Reb Shlomo Zalman demanded. "I would like to see him and discuss the matter with him personally."

The couple hurriedly honored Reb Shlomo Zalman's request and brought their son before the sage.

"What is your name, my boy?" the Gaon asked.

"Akiva," the child replied.

"How do you do, Akiva. My name is Shlomo Zalman. I am the *Gadol Ha-dor*, the greatest Torah authority of this generation, and everyone listens to me. You are going to enter a special school now, and I would like you to represent me and look after all of the religious matters in your new home."

The boy's eyes were riveted to the Gaon's face, and the awestruck parents sat with their mouths agape as the Rav continued. "I shall now give you *semichah,* which makes you a rabbi, and I want you to use this honor wisely."

Reb Shlomo Zalman gently stroked the child's cheek and saw that he was as eager as could be to fulfill his part of the agreement. Over the years, on numerous occasions when this youngster was to spend a Shabbos at home, he refused to leave the institution, insisting that as the local rabbi he had a responsibility to his constituents. After all, he had been charged with this responsibility by none other than the *Gadol Ha-dor*!

Judgments Sweeter than Honey

EB SHLOMO ZALMAN'S mastery of *Shulchan Aruch* evoked the admiration and esteem of all. Unlike other great scholars, he did not have a particular forte or specialty; he was proficient in every facet of the four volumes of the Code of Jewish Law. Yet some have pointed out that Reb Shlomo Zalman's most outstanding expertise was in the area known colloquially as "The fifth volume of *Shulchan Aruch*," meaning *sechel*. This innate intelligence and intuitive

sense was evident in each of Reb Shlomo Zalman's rulings. His halachic decisions were classics of innovation, responsibility, and leadership.

This celebrated facet of the Gaon's erudition was, as one *Rosh Yeshivah* noted ruefully, the facet least imitated. Were *b'nei Torah* to properly observe how he employed "The fifth volume of *Shulchan Aruch*," the situation and the image of yeshiva students would vastly improve.

❃ ❃ ❃

When doubts arose regarding the parentage of a particular new immigrant to Israel, the young man turned to Rabbi Baruch Dov Povarsky, dean of the Ponevezh Yeshiva, who investigated his case thoroughly and communicated his findings to the leading halachic authorities. Their decision would have enormous implications in the immigrant's life, for if his Judaism was suspect, he could not receive the Rabbinate's permission to marry a Jewish woman; he could not be called to the Torah; he could not be counted in a minyan or buried in a Jewish cemetery. It was found that the young man was indeed a Jew (and would not even require *giyur mi-safek*) and various authorities issued rulings to this effect.

Reb Shlomo Zalman was not satisfied with simply deciding the case: the ramifications of the decision were too great. He therefore announced that he wished to personally officiate at the young man's wedding, and indeed he did. Concerning this incident, Rabbi Povarsky declared, "There is *psak*, and there is *PSAK*!"

❊ ❊ ❊

A very bright young lady with cerebral palsy, who was confined to a wheelchair, had been able to achieve a remarkable degree of independence. Her apartment was tailored to her special needs and her battery powered wheelchair provided mobility all week long. On Shabbos, however, when the use of her automatic wheelchair was forbidden, the girl was confined to her home.

When her parents heard about a uniquely designed wheelchair produced by the Tzomet Institute, they decided to look into it. At Tzomet, as at the Institute of Science and Halachah, men of science and *b'nei Torah* join forces to produce innovative devices for contemporary living that conform to the demands of Halachah. The apparatus in question, a *"grama"* wheelchair, operates in a manner that violates no prohibitions on Shabbos and Yom

Tov. The parents were enthusiastic, but this young woman, despite her difficulty in life, could not overcome her discomfort with using this device. She was well aware of the fact that she had been dealt a great challenge in life and she intended to meet it without relying on what she viewed as lenient dispensations.

While her intentions, of course, were as noble as they were pious, they resulted in her entire family spending Shabbos cooped up in their apartment, attending to her needs and keeping her company.

When Reb Shlomo Zalman became aware of the young lady's situation he informed her that for her, using the *grama* wheelchair was by no means a *b'diavad* — an *a posteriori* (an action that was permitted after the fact). So strong were his feelings on the matter that he said he was even willing to have a *hechsher* attached to the back of the chair, stating that he personally approved its use on Shabbos.

Reb Shlomo Zalman ruled that, contrary to common practice, it is unnecessary to fill a Kiddush cup or *kos shel berachah* to the very top. Basing his opinion on a Talmudic source, the Gaon maintained that provided that the cup contains a *revi'is*, the required minimum for Kiddush, filling it to the brim might even be counterproductive. To fill a cup to the brim and then hand it to someone else who will inevitably spill it, is certainly no honor for the person or the blessing.

Once at a wedding where the Gaon was officiating, an attendant began to decant a full cup of wine under the *chuppah*, but Reb Shlomo Zalman interrupted him, saying, "Personally, I don't mind if you are *machmir*, but you should not be stringent at the expense of the bride's gown..."

❊ ❊ ❊

When a married student passed away, his family had to make a quick decision about where he should be buried. They had the option of selecting a single plot that was available in an area of the cemetery where some of their distinguished ancestors were interred, or alternatively, they could purchase a double plot in a different area, so that after one hundred and twenty, his widow could be laid to rest in the vacant site adjacent to his.

They consulted Reb Shlomo Zalman who, without any hesitation, ruled that the student should be buried in the single plot near his ancestors and relatives. The "*sechel* factor," it seems, contributed significantly to the Rav's decision. His rationale, as he later explained, was that buying the double plot would place an unfair emotional burden upon the young widow: The poor woman had every right to remarry; however, if there were a burial plot waiting for her alongside her deceased husband, she would always be plagued with the thought that perhaps it was inappropriate for her to remarry. She would feel she had a commitment to her husband, to lie at his side after one hundred and twenty.

An aging bachelor who was becoming, day by day and year by year, less and less eligible, had additional shortcomings that made finding a match for him all the more difficult. He had stipulated that he would consider only a girl who was prepared to care for his elderly and ailing mother, and allow her to live in their home once they were wed. Needless to say, this precondition did nothing to enhance his opportunities or endear him to prospective candidates, and fewer and fewer offers were being made to him.

Reb Shlomo Zalman's in-laws, Rabbi Aryeh Leib and Sarah Ruchamkin,זצ"ל. The Gaon lived in their humble abode in Shaarei Chesed and cared for the elderly Rebbetzin until she passed to her final reward. He treated her with the utmost respect and honored her deeply.

Photo circa 1949, when Reb Shlomo Zalman first became dean of Kol Torah.

Reb Shlomo Zalman and his family, circa 1936. Front row: Avraham Dov (presently Rav and Rosh Kollel of Tiberias), Rochel (today wife of Harav Zalman Nechemiah Goldberg), and Shmuel (currently Rosh Yeshivah of Ma'alos Ha Torah).

The sisters of Reb Shlomo Zalman.
Back row (l. to r.): Rebbetzin Leah Schwadron, ע״ה*, Rebbetzin Malka Hurwitz,* ע״ה
Center: תבלחט״י*, Rebbetzin Rochel Laizerzon,*
Front row: Rebbetzin Sarah Prague.

Speaking with R. Elya Lopian, זצ״ל, (l.).

(R to l.) Rabbis Yaakov Moshe Charlop, Issar Zalman Meltzer, Dov Weidenfeld (of Tchabin) זצ״ל. Three gaonim who had a profound influence upon Reb Shlomo Zalman.

The Rav never stopped teaching.

On the occasion of the publication of an important sefer. Among those pictured: Harav Yaakov Yitzchak Weiss, זצ"ל; ליבחלי"ח, Rabbi Yisroel Moshe Dushinsky, Rabbi Moshe Halberstam, שליט"א.

With Reb Shmuel Auerbach, שליט״א.

At the wedding of Reb Ezriel, with Reb Yosef Shalom Elyashiv, שליט״א, and Reb Elyashiv's brother-in-law, Reb Shmuel Aaron Yudelevitch, זצ״ל.

*At Kol Torah. Reb Shlomo Zalman's
love of learning was contagious.*

My beloved Rebbe graced many of my family's joyous occasions.

The bachelor's relatives were up in arms over his precondition. Even without it, they reasoned, it was not as if the young ladies were breaking down his door, and the stipulation all but guaranteed that the prospects wouldn't even knock politely. "Your only hope," they assured him repeatedly, "is to have your mother admitted to an old age home, where she will get professional care."

Due to the mounting and relentless pressure that the family had imposed, the bachelor reluctantly turned to Reb Shlomo Zalman Auerbach and presented his situation. The Rav heard his visitor out and then told him that he heartily agreed with the stipulation. The Gaon contended that the most important thing about a prospective wife was her good character, and her willingness to accept such a difficult condition would attest to the fact that she was imbued with wonderful *middos tovos*. Furthermore, if after marrying a girl who did not meet this criterion, his mother had to be placed in an old age home, the new husband would forever hold it against his wife, thinking that because of her heartless inconsideration his poor mother had to live out her years among strangers.

Armed with the Gaon's confirmation, the bachelor continued to adhere to his inflexible precondition. It appeared that Reb Shlomo Zalman had not only rendered a ruling but also a blessing, for soon after the encounter, the not-so-young man returned to the Rav to tell him the delightful news that he was finally engaged to be married.

Reb Shlomo Zalman was overjoyed. "Now you know for sure that you have a woman with gilt-edged qualities," the Rav declared. "And now, too, the time has come for you to make arrangements for your mother in a good old age home. It is far too much responsibility for a young wife to have to bear such a burden..."

Many in a particular American Jewish community wished to have an *eruv* erected,* but the project from the outset was fraught with halachic and political disputes. Attempts at mediation and compromise failed and in

---

* An *eruv* is a halachic device which in effect encloses an area comprised of public and private domains, rendering it permissible to carry items from one domain to the other on Shabbos. To create this enclosure in a neighborhood, often a wire is strung between posts driven into the ground in a pattern that encircles the area.

Judgments Sweeter than Honey / 139

the end, the *eruv* was being built on a powder keg. The subject was destined to explode the image of harmony which this community formerly projected.

One *Posek* offered the following solution: The *eruv* could be used by the women, but the men should refrain from relying upon it. When this ruling was brought to Reb Shlomo Zalman's attention, he reacted with uncommon vehemence. "Men recite the blessing, 'for not having made me a woman'," he said, "and women recite the blessing, 'for having made me according to His will.' But both genders recite the blessing 'for not having made me a gentile...' What kind of *psak* is this?" The Gaon's frustration was manifest. "The *eruv* is either good for every Jew or good for no Jew — there should be no distinction made between men and women. The community should see to it that it is good for all."

One Sunday morning Reb Shlomo Zalman gathered his students at Kol Torah and told them: "A terrible thing happened in my neighborhood and I must make you aware of it." The students cowered in anticipation of the dire news the Gaon was about to deliver. Everyone knew how deeply Reb Shlomo Zalman was involved in easing the plight of orphans and widows, and every tragic case in Israel and abroad seemed to reach his sympathetic ear. If their Rav, who never revealed the *tzaros* that he encountered, wished now to relate a terrible event that had transpired, one could only imagine the gravity of the situation.

The seriousness of Reb Shlomo Zalman's disposition and the somber tone of his voice only served to intensify their fear that the event was even more horrendous than their vivid imaginations could conjure up. A hush of trepidation fell over the study hall as the Gaon began to speak.

Reb Shlomo Zalman related that on Shabbos he had seen a man dragging benches to the shul for a collation in honor of his son's engagement. The man's son, who was walking at his side, did not so much as lift a finger to help his father. "I could not contain my bewilderment," the Rav told his listeners, "and I asked the *chassan* to explain why his father was doing all of the shlepping. He proudly explained that even where there was an *eruv*, he himself did not carry on Shabbos and was therefore unable to lend a hand."

This reply enraged the Rav. The very idea of so-called religiosity taking precedence over honoring one's father was anathema to him. The young man could easily have avoided this situation with any number of possible solutions, without violating the custom he had adopted. The Gaon viewed this as a prime example of distorted logic.

Reb Shlomo Zalman appreciated a direct approach and straight thinking. He had little patience for twisted reasoning and even less for chicanery, and he never sought avenues or loopholes within Halachah that might lead to less-than-honest behavior. He detested the reliance on such loopholes. He maintained that if one becomes accustomed to (permissible) cheating, the attribute will be imbued in his soul and begin to take control. Cheating, even when licensed by some Halachic escape clause, will become his standard operating procedure, and one step will lead to the next on a downward spiral to iniquity. Therefore, one must constantly guard one's soul and always be perfectly straight and honest.

A senior member of Israel's secret service (Mossad) became religious at precisely the same time that he was recommended for an extended espionage mission in an Arab country. The clandestine mission was potentially of enormous value for Israel's security and could theoretically save countless lives.

The newly religious agent found himself impaled on the horns of a dilemma. On the one hand, if he were to accept this mission it would be the high point of his career and his greatest contribution to his people. On the other hand, embarking on such a mission would inevitably entail violating virtually every religious precept and tenet that he had come to value.

The agent brought his *she'elah* to Reb Shlomo Zalman, and explained that for the duration of the time that he would be abroad he would have to live as a gentile. There would be no observing Shabbos and kashrus, no laying of *tefillin* — in fact nothing that would so much as hint at his Jewish identity.

The Gaon began by saying that for such a mission, it was an obligation to accept the assignment. The inevitable violation of mitzvas was a sad but unavoidable consequence, the price one must pay for the privilege and obligation of protecting one's brethren. This was no different, he said, from what Esther had done. She too had to sacrifice her religious observances in order to save her people.

"Furthermore," the Rav continued, "I do not believe that this would have a detrimental effect upon one's religiosity. Once the mission is accomplished, God willing, one would be able to return home and resume a lifestyle that is religious and pure.

"However, despite all these compelling reasons, I do not recommend that *you* accept this mission, for I am afraid of one thing: Any man who accepts such an assignment and is willing to live at such peril, must also be prepared to kill in an instant, without compunction. This is the nature of espionage, and the likely by-product will be that the act of shedding blood will become 'insignificant in your eyes.' Once a person sheds another human being's blood, his value system begins to erode and becomes corrupted, and he becomes able to follow up an assassination with a leisurely cup of coffee. *You* will not be able to rectify this kind of damage to your soul after the mission is over."

Karen, an assimilated college student vacationing in Israel, had inadvertently stumbled across her religion and started attending a few classes to find out more about Judaism. The attendance of classes, of course, cannot be confused with adopting a religious lifestyle, and Karen was still in the very initial stages of discovering what Torah and mitzvas were all about.

One day Karen ever-so-casually mentioned to a friend of hers that she was pregnant and was going to have an abortion. This friend brought the matter to the attention of Rabbi Stein in Jerusalem, whom Karen had become acquainted with over the previous few days.

Rabbi Stein was naturally upset when he heard this, but what could he say to dissuade a "liberated" young woman raised on a cultural doctrine of "Do your own thing" and "It's *my* body and I'll do with it as I please," a woman who had yet to learn what a mitzva *was*, let alone the obligation to observe it.

In a last-ditch effort, Rabbi Stein devised the following scheme: He explained to Karen that having this procedure close to the end of the first trimester was by no means free of risk. It was therefore incumbent upon her, he said, to seek the blessing of a "holy man" before undergoing the operation, and Karen saw no reason to object.

Rabbi Stein brought the young woman to see Reb Shlomo Zalman, and it goes without saying that his intention was anything but to get the Gaon's blessing for this venture. When the two were ushered into the Rav's study, Rabbi Stein provided the Gaon with a brief synopsis of the situation and then remained to serve as interpreter.

Reb Shlomo Zalman then asked Karen why she had come to see him. Karen replied that she was there to seek his blessing. The Rav asked, "A blessing for what?" and Karen explained that she was about to have her pregnancy terminated and since this procedure involved some danger she sought the great Rabbi's blessing for success, safety, and good health.

Reb Shlomo Zalman, however, was not swift in dispensing his blessing. First some questions had to be answered. "Why is it that you want this procedure done?"

Karen explained that she was planning to embark on a long course of study toward the career which she had chosen, and having a baby would only get in her way.

"What sort of career do you intend to pursue?" the Rav asked.

"I want to be a doctor," the young woman replied.

"I see," the Gaon remarked. "And why do you want to be a doctor?"

Karen launched into the standard speech of a medical school applicant, explaining that there was nothing more noble or altruistic than the field of medicine.

"And why is it," Reb Shlomo Zalman inquired, "that you hold medicine in such high esteem?"

"Why," she exclaimed, taken aback at having to explain all this to a man of supposed intelligence and stature, "through medicine one is able to save lives!" The irony of her response apparently escaped her.

The Gaon just sat in his chair contemplating her answer, as if it were a revolutionary concept and a challenging one for him to grasp. Karen began to get a little fidgety. She could not understand what the difficulty was. Gears and cogs that should have been meshing in her head appeared to be jammed in some kind of cerebral gridlock that prevented them from making the simple connections from one synapse to another.

Finally, after what seemed an eternity of cogitation, he asked the young mother-to-be, "What is so important about saving lives?"

Karen was stumped. Not at the answer — why, everyone knew that there *was* no greater value — but at this purportedly brilliant Rabbi's inability to comprehend something so elementary. She glanced at her interpreter to verify that she had understood him. Then she glanced at him to verify that *he* had understood *her*.

Once she discerned that Reb Shlomo Zalman was in fact waiting for an answer to the question of why saving lives was so important, she let him have it: "There simply is nothing more important in the whole world. In the universe!"

The Gaon reflected on this as well, giving his guest time to let it all sink in. But still the cogs and gears were not turning.

Finally Karen woke up and smelled the coffee. "Oh, no," she said with a start. "This," she declared, pointing at her abdomen, "this is only a fetus, not a life."

Reb Shlomo Zalman awarded her a quizzical look. He made it clear that he was not clear about the distinction between a fetus and a life. "But you do agree," he asked most accommodatingly, "that a fetus will become a baby?"

Karen couldn't deny that, but she still maintained that currently it was not yet a life.

To this the Gaon asked, "What if I were to tell you that your baby is destined to become a great person?"

It did not take Karen long to respond. "There is no way of knowing if the baby would or would not become a great person."

"True," Reb Shlomo Zalman agreed, appreciating her reply, "but you have only answered half the question. Why is it that there is no way of knowing how the baby will develop?"

"Because there are so many factors involved. Genetics, geography, nutrition, environmental influences, and so forth. It's basically a question of 'nature versus nurture'."

"But you certainly realize the kind of input that you as a mother and an intelligent person could have." Karen readily conceded this point.

"I am sure," the Rav asserted, "that the child will be bright, for you seem to be a clever individual. So the 'nature' is there; the factor that is in doubt is the surroundings, the role that the environment will play upon this child's upbringing.

"I therefore believe," Reb Shlomo Zalman continued with certitude, "that there are but two courses for you to follow with this child: Either you raise it, and nurture the baby with the love that it deserves and that you could certainly provide; or you give it to me. My name is Shlomo Zalman Auerbach, and you can ask around — I am pretty well-known. I would be glad to see to it that your baby would not be denied the nurturing it deserves. But these are clearly the only two choices you have."

Karen repeated after him, as if reciting a mantra, "The only two choices, the only two choices...," Her brow furrowed, she seemed to fold inward into stony silence. At last she asked, "Do I have to make that decision now?"

Rabbi Stein could hardly believe the *question*. In a matter of two minutes Reb Shlomo Zalman, one unschooled in the methodology of *kiruv rechokim* and never briefed on how to zero in on the wavelength of a college kid devoid of a religious background, had accomplished the ultimate in auto-suggestion, as it is known. He had allowed her — a young woman who had merely come to seek a blessing before a "minor" clinical procedure — to figure out for herself that she really had only *one* choice: to have the baby. The Gaon had deftly maneuvered the conversation so that she had come to this conclusion on her own. Whether to keep her child or give him to a perfect stranger was, at this point, a question not even worthy of a question mark.

[Author's note: The outcome of this encounter is a bright young lady who will soon be enrolled in a Bais Yaakov Teachers' Seminary.]

❋ ❋ ❋

Judgments Sweeter than Honey / 151

The joy the Levinsohns experienced at the birth of their second child was quickly dampened when the attending pediatrician informed them that their baby had numerous, and serious, complications. The series of tests performed over the following weeks proved that none of the doctor's fears had been groundless. Their baby's life appeared to be hanging by a gossamer thread that was in the process of unraveling. Like all parents in such a predicament, they consulted with numerous specialists and medical experts. Some of the authorities informed the Levinsohns that a treatment available abroad had had a degree of success in saving the lives of infants with problems like their newborn's. However, this life-saving treatment, which was neither inexpensive nor guaranteed, would do nothing to alleviate the chronic conditions with which this poor little soul was afflicted.

The physicians at the hospital were opposed to sending the baby abroad. They advised the distraught parents to pursue a *laissez faire* policy and allow nature to run its course.

The awesome responsibility of that decision was too weighty for this couple to bear and so they, like countless others, placed it on the broad shoulders of Reb Shlomo Zalman Auerbach.

The Rav was not impressed with the doctors' scheme of passive infanticide and proposed an altogether different plan of action: "There is a special *malach*," he explained very patiently, "a Heavenly Being who watches over babies and children." He cited numerous examples to prove his point, such as the fact that toddlers often ingest dirt and other inedibles and yet continue to function normally, showing no ill effects, while an adult who would do this would most likely suffer a serious illness — at the very least! Children seem to thrive even in the absence of sanitary conditions, whereas adults more readily succumb to diseases such as typhus and hepatitis. Youngsters have been known to fall from great heights — out of open windows or off playground equipment — and escape unscathed.

"Accordingly, I propose the following idea: You *daven* for your son and I will *daven* for him, and let us give the Almighty a chance to intervene..."

The parents were very relieved to accept the Rav's suggestion...and far more relieved from the *nachas* their problem-free miracle baby, now a strapping bar mitzva *bachur*, brings them.

A newly observant woman who had attended many classes covering a range of Jewish topics, including the Halachic standards of modesty, confessed to her rabbi that she had a problem. She wanted to observe all of the mitzvas, but one of them was simply too hard for her.

She explained that, since she had once been married, she was required to cover her hair. Her lifestyle, however, made this extremely inconvenient, to say the least. She was a career woman and she still worked at the same place she was working at before she had become religious. After all of the changes that had occurred in her life since discovering religion, changes which had been hard enough for her and her colleagues to adjust to, she couldn't just show up one day at work with a head covering. Such a dramatic alteration in her appearance would mandate an explanation, and this would mean revealing embarrassing information regarding her past, about which she preferred to remain discreet. Her rabbi listened with understanding to her plight, but humiliation notwithstanding, he saw no solution. The Halachah, at least as he understood it, required her to cover her hair.

The rabbi told her that situations such as this require consultation with an expert in Halachah. He would confer with Reb Shlomo Zalman Auerbach, he said, and report his decision to her.

Reb Shlomo Zalman ruled that, for now, *this* woman, who was still new at mitzva observance, should wear a head covering for all matters of sanctity, such as prayer in the synagogue, etc. At other times, when her circumstances precluded doing so, it was permissible for *her* not to cover her hair.

The rabbi who had posed the question suggested that since there were wigs today that looked so natural that few would ever realize they were not the wearer's natural hair, the woman might use one of them for a head covering.

Reb Shlomo Zalman looked at the rabbi for a moment and then responded as only he could: "You do not know, nor do you have any way of knowing, how this woman would feel with a wig — which she considers a source of embarrassment — on her head."

Judgments Sweeter than Honey / 155

The Gaon's decision in hand, the rabbi returned to the woman and reported all that had transpired, including his own suggestion and Reb Shlomo Zalman's dismissal of it. The woman was so taken by the Rav's sensitivity that she decided then and there that from that day onward she would cover her hair at all times!

❋ ❋ ❋

One day Rabbi Yosef Buxbaum drove the Rav to pay a condolence call. As the house was situated on a very narrow street, Rabbi Buxbaum parked the car on the sidewalk so that it would not impede traffic, and then hurried around to help the Gaon alight.

The space between the parked car and the wall of the adjacent apartment building was so tight, however, that Rabbi Buxbaum found himself wedged between a rock and a hard place, and while extricating himself, his suit jacket tore.

Reb Shlomo Zalman sensed at once that something was amiss. He ordered Rabbi Buxbaum to stand still while he examined him.

The honorable driver had no idea what Reb Shlomo Zalman intended. The Rav peered wordlessly at the rip in the material, inspecting the extent of the damage. Rabbi Buxbaum, unaccustomed to the role of model, was even less accustomed to Reb Shlomo Zalman's interest in matters sartorial.

But it seems that even a torn suit jacket falls in the purview of Halachic adjudication. After sizing up the situation, the Gaon ruled that Rabbi Buxbaum could not enter the home of the bereaved wearing a tattered coat. Rabbi Buxbaum protested, but Reb Shlomo Zalman cited the Halachic principal that honoring God's creations takes precedence over comforting mourners.

Rabbi Buxbaum quickly tucked the ripped part of the jacket into his pocket so that it was no longer noticeable, and asked the Rav if they could now get on with their *shivah* call. Reb Shlomo Zalman was not yet convinced. He insisted that Rabbi Buxbaum walk a few paces down the block and up again so that he might determine if the damage was indeed invisible. Only when he was completely satisfied that it was, did he allow the condolence visit to proceed as planned.

❊ ❊ ❊

Judgments Sweeter than Honey / 157

A gentleman came to ask Reb Shlomo Zalman a *she'elah* regarding the placement of a *mezuzah* in his house. But try as he might to describe the traffic pattern in the house — which door was the main entrance and which was the secondary access — clarity failed to be achieved. The Rav had no recourse. He donned his coat and got ready to go and inspect the premises firsthand.

The man was appalled at the trouble to which he was about to subject Reb Shlomo Zalman. Indeed, he protested vehemently, "I didn't come here to make the Rav trek out to my house!"

But the Gaon quickly corrected his visitor. "I'm not going there to see you — I'm going to see your *mezuzah*."

Years ago, there was a couple in Jerusalem who had not been blessed with a child. After seeing several specialists, Mr. and Mrs. Levine turned to Israel's greatest authority in the field, Professor Bernard Zondek. Professor Zondek informed the couple that there was a new treatment that might help them but it was only available abroad. (Today Israel is the leading country in successful treatment of problems in this area.)

In those days it was virtually unheard of to raise money for someone to travel overseas for medical treatment. The few instances in which this had been done were all life-threatening emergencies. The prospects of the Levines being able to raise funds for their trip were therefore very slim, and the expenses they would incur would be astronomical. Aside from the actual medical expenses, the course of their treatment might involve their being away for a year without any income, and there was the high price of living abroad to contend with.

Despite the exorbitant costs involved, the Levines desperately wanted to have a family. Mr. Levine sat down with pen and paper to calculate how two Israeli moderate-salaried employees could ever afford to embark on this odyssey. Clearly their limited resources would barely cover their air fare. But they did have one asset, Mr. Levine concluded, and it would have to be liquidated. Yes, their humble apartment would have to go on the market.

Mrs. Levine reluctantly agreed to this drastic step. In her heart of hearts she realized there was no alternative. Nonetheless, she felt that before they went any further they should acquire the blessing of Reb Shlomo Zalman. Mr. Levine concurred.

He went to see the Rav and presented the problem *and* his solution. But after hearing Mr. Levine's rendition, Reb Shlomo Zalman disagreed with the plan. "You are willing to undertake such enormous expense," he asked, "so that you might fulfill the mitzva of being fruitful?"

Mr. Levine nodded.

"But your plan does not conform to Halachic parameters. The Halachah prohibits expending more than a fifth of one's income in order to fulfill a positive commandment. The amount you intend to spend is far in excess of that."

At first Mr. Levine thought that Reb Shlomo Zalman was engaging in pilpulistic reasoning, which ignored their problem and their plight. Little did he realize that the Gaon was setting the stage for a miracle, within the framework of Halachah.

Reb Shlomo Zalman repeated his objection. "If you indeed wish to perform this mitzva then you must do it in accordance with

Halachah. Otherwise, instead of performing a mitzva you would be doing something that is prohibited. Your goal and desire are one hundred percent correct, but your method of achieving that goal must comply with the *Shulchan Aruch*."

Rather than leave them with only his objection, however, the Gaon suggested an alternate plan: "I recently heard about a new doctor at Bikur Cholim Hospital who is supposed to have a good reputation in these areas," he said. "Why don't you try him? And, needless to say, you should also *daven* with the utmost sincerity."

Recommending a new doctor instead of Professor Zondek would be comparable to recommending a first-grade arithmetic teacher in place of a university professor of Advanced Mathematics. But nevertheless, Mr. Levine was prepared to accept the Rav's ruling, if only the Rav would agree to *daven* as well. Reb Shlomo Zalman readily accepted the partnership.

One year later Reb Shlomo Zalman was invited to be a *sandek* at Junior Levine's bris.

❋ ❋ ❋

A student approached Reb Shlomo Zalman on behalf of a friend, to ask an unusual *she'elah*. The friend wanted to know how many fast days he should accept upon himself in order to rectify a wrongdoing.

Reb Shlomo Zalman told the young man that he had to convince his friend not to accept *any* fast days upon himself. "Nowadays," the Rav said, "fasts can, and usually do, lead to sadness, and sadness is the very root of impurity. If your friend is married, the crime of fasting can become felonious, for when he comes home to break his fast, if the food is not ready for him, he might become angry with his wife, and once he gets angry — for any cause — then whatever benefit there was to his fasting is outweighed by the loss."

But the young man persisted. "What should I tell my friend, then?" he asked. "He very much wants to fast."

Reb Shlomo Zalman reiterated that he would be best advised, especially if he was indeed a friend, to convince the fellow not to engage in fasting. However, if he remains adamant, then he should refrain from eating two of his favorite dishes for a month's time, and no longer than that.

Again, the young man stubbornly refused to accept the Gaon's reply. "My friend will feel that his question wasn't answered," he objected.

"Well, then," Reb Shlomo Zalman responded with a shrug of his shoulders, "if you cannot get him to do any of the above, and he is still bent on fasting, then have him fast Mondays and Thursdays during the month of Elul — until midday."

An Israeli army chaplain, after a brief but highly successful military career, sought to leave the army and become a *Rosh Yeshivah*. The top brass were very displeased with the chaplain's decision and they tried in every possible way to dissuade this "major" asset from hanging up his uniform. They told him that they were prepared to offer him a compromise deal whereby he could spend some time each day in the army and devote the rest to delivering lectures in a yeshiva.

The chaplain brought his question to the dean of a Hesder yeshiva, and explained that while he could not deny that he was making a contribution to the army, he felt, or certainly feared, that his own spirituality would suffer were he not to take a full-time position outside of the army framework.

This *Rosh Yeshivah* responded, תורה מה לי הכא מה לי התם —"Here or there, Torah is Torah [and therefore you do not lose out by remaining in the army]." After receiving this reply, the chaplain, still unsure, sought the opinion of Reb Shlomo Zalman.

The Gaon listened carefully to all the factors and then ruled: "*Chayecha kodmin* — your life takes precedence over the lives of others. You are not obliged to sacrifice your own spirituality, or place it in jeopardy, even in such a situation."

At this point, the chaplain quoted the Hesder *Rosh Yeshivah*'s opinion.

Reb Shlomo Zalman nodded and said, " The *Rosh Yeshivah* is correct."

The chaplain looked at the Rav uncomprehendingly, for this was an absolute contradiction. First, the Rav had ruled that he was not obliged to put his own spirituality in peril, and now the Rav was concurring with the *Rosh Yeshivah* who had claimed that there was no difference between a Torah-oriented life within the army chaplaincy framework and a Torah-oriented life within a yeshiva framework.

The chaplain begged for an explanation, which the Gaon was happy to provide: "If this *Rosh Yeshivah* feels that there is no difference between the army and the yeshiva, then he should switch places with you. You will become the *Rosh Yeshivah* and let *him* be the chaplain."

Designated Driver

I T WAS ONLY a half-hour bus ride from the Yeshiva in Bayit Vegan to the Machaneh Yehudah outdoor market, and a mere twenty-minute walk from there to his modest home in Shaarei Chesed. So why should Reb Shlomo Zalman burden Kol Torah with the expense of a taxi fare or impose upon anyone to drive him? Public transportation was inexpensive, reliable, and more than adequate, as far as the *Rosh Yeshivah* was concerned. Thus for many years Reb Shlomo Zalman, despite the vehement protests of the Yeshiva administration and the heartfelt pleas of those who sought the privilege of driving the Gaon, rode the bus just like any other "*posheter Yid*" — as he frequently referred to himself.

Stories abound in Jerusalem about this "Simple Jew," the *tzaddik* on the bus — such as the time Reb Shlomo Zalman remained in his seat for several blocks beyond his regular stop, so as not to disturb the woman in the aisle seat who was laden with packages and shopping baskets. It is fairly likely that such actions were commonplace for a *Gadol* noted for his humility. In his later years, however, Reb Shlomo Zalman did relent and allow a taxi to be routinely ordered for him from the Hapisga Taxi Company located near the Yeshiva.

There is no dearth of yeshivas in Bayit Vegan, nor of *Rashei Yeshivah*. Indeed Jerusalem has the greatest concentration of yeshivas in history, but the honor and privilege of ferrying the *Posek Ha-dor* to and from his Torah academy was highly valued among the Hapisga drivers. So much so, in fact, that they frequently vied among themselves for this *zechus*.

Rabbi Rafael Wolpin relates that once, when riding in a cab, he was surprised to hear the lively strains of chassidic music emanating from the driver's tape deck. The cabbie, with his sports shirt agape, gold chain necklaces nestling among his chest hair, and full head of curly tresses bare of any head covering, seemed an unlikely fan of Benzion Shenker, and yet he was nodding and tapping along with the stirring rhythms.

When Rabbi Wolpin asked him how he had come by this particular cassette, the driver was proud to relate that his "rabbi" had given it to him. "Have you heard of Reb Shlomo Zalman?" he inquired of his passenger. "Well, I'm his regular driver. Once, I suppose the tape I had on was bothering him, so he gave me this one to play instead. I've treasured it ever since — do you like it?"

Another cabbie at Hapisga noted that Reb Shlomo Zalman always sat up front, alongside the driver, instead of in the back seat. "I sensed that he didn't want me to feel like his servant or his chauffeur, you know?" the cabbie said. "And he'd talk to me the whole way, asking me questions about my family and like that. Imagine, *me* — talking to Reb Shlomo Zalman like he was just an ordinary passenger!" This cabbie, like all the others at Hapisga, proudly claimed the honor of having been Reb Shlomo Zalman's "regular driver."

Rabbi Yehoshua Neuwirth relates that Reb Shlomo Zalman believed that money was not adequate compensation for favors and services; it was essential to also treat the provider of such services with extreme courtesy and show a genuine interest in their work and in them as individuals. Incapable of engaging in meaningless small talk, Reb Shlomo Zalman would raise a general topic and somehow manage to make the conversation elevating to the listener. Once, in a smoke-filled taxi, the topic of conversation was how to break the smoking habit.

"I've tried to quit a million times," the driver said, "but it's no use. I just keep coming back to it."

"I do not understand," Reb Shlomo Zalman replied. "What is the difficulty? I myself was once a heavy smoker but after hearing from my doctor that it was causing me serious harm, I sat down and weighed the pleasure I received from smoking against the inherent dangers and concluded that I must stop. Immediately. And as a matter of fact, from that moment to this I have never smoked another cigarette."

The dispatcher at Hapisga had this to add: "One day I was taking my turn behind the wheel and I picked up Reb Shlomo Zalman over at Kol Torah. As usual, he climbed into the front seat and greeted me, calling me his *manhig*. I tried to explain to him that in Hebrew the word for 'driver' is *nahag* and that although the two words have the same root, *manhig* means 'leader.' I figured he was more accustomed to speaking Yiddish, so he wasn't aware of the subtleties of Hebrew grammar. But no — Reb Shlomo Zalman insisted that I was his *manhig* because I would 'lead' him to his destination. It was such a small thing, and yet it made me feel great. This important Rabbi considered me his *manhig*!"

Among the hundreds of thousands of mourners at Reb Shlomo Zalman Auerbach's funeral was a contingent of *manhigim* from the Hapisga Taxi Company — each and every one of them his "regular driver."

When Reb Shlomo Zalman finally relented and allowed himself to be driven to wherever he needed to go, it was Reb Yosef Buxbaum who earned the privilege of being one of the first "designated drivers."

It was not long after he had acquired his driving license that Rabbi Buxbaum was asked to take Reb Shlomo Zalman to a wedding. As the affair was to be held outside of Jerusalem and the *chuppah* was scheduled for five-thirty, Rabbi Buxbaum and his esteemed passenger agreed that they would leave at four o'clock.

In those days there was only one telephone in the entire Shaarei Chesed neighborhood and that was in Rabbi Buxbaum's house, so when his driver failed to arrive on schedule, there was nothing the Rav could do but continue to wait and wonder what had caused the delay. It could not have been due to Rabbi Buxbaum's having lost his way, he considered, and it was unlikely that the *talmid* had forgotten this appointment. After all, he had practically begged for the so-called honor, and in addition, they had made the arrangement only twenty-four hours before. Perhaps Reb Yosef, still inexperienced, was having trouble with his car?

While Reb Shlomo Zalman waited, growing progressively anxious, Rabbi Buxbaum waited too, until the hands of his watch approached four-thirty. He had made a simple calculation: If they were to leave at four o'clock as planned, Reb Shlomo Zalman would be one of the earliest arrivals at the wedding, and that — to the new driver's mind — would not be appropriate. Everyone knows that weddings do not begin on time, he told himself, and for the Gaon to stand around waiting for everyone else to arrive before the wedding began would be an affront to his honor.

When Rabbi Buxbaum arrived at the Auerbach home at four-thirty, to his great surprise he was greeted by a rather cross Reb Shlomo Zalman. In response to the Rav's question, "What kept you?" Rabbi Buxbaum explained his reasoning and assured the *Rosh Yeshivah* that he had acted in his best interests.

Reb Shlomo Zalman saw things quite differently. "There are so many things a bridegroom has on his mind," Reb Shlomo Zalman admonished his student. "There are countless worries, aggravated by the fact that he is fasting too. One of his concerns is that the rabbi who is performing the ceremony arrive on time. I am to be the *mesader kiddushin* there — and I cannot bear the thought of my contributing to the *chassan's* anxiety.

"I do not mind arriving half an hour early," he went on. "I can sit on the side and not be a bother to anyone. Anything is better than adding to the bridegroom's worries. So, listen to me, Reb Yosef — this is the first time that we are riding together. I will not hold it against you if you choose to never drive me again, but if you do, the time we agree upon must be the time, and not a minute later."

The Ways
of the Righteous

ON THE FRONT PORCH of their Shaarei Chesed apartment, Reb Shlomo Zalman and his Rebbetzin relaxed after their Shabbos repast. This was a fixed part of their weekly routine, a few minutes of light conversation before Reb Shlomo Zalman would excuse himself and retire to his study to learn.

The Rebbetzin, however, would remain at her post, leisurely taking in the sights. From time to time, if she observed something noteworthy, she would call out, "Shlomo Zalman!" in order to share the sight with her beloved husband. No matter what Reb Shlomo Zalman was learning at that moment, even if he were in the midst of the most complex *sugya*, as soon as he heard his wife's voice calling he was there. The Rebbetzin would point out the curiosity and he would dutifully take a peek, sometimes offering an approving comment such as, "Very nice." After a nod of agreement he would immediately return to his learning.

The degree of honor that Reb Shlomo Zalman afforded his wife was greater than that afforded to kings. This is not merely a metaphorical analogy, but the testimony of family members and neighbors alike.

When Rabbi Yosef Buxbaum celebrated his fiftieth birthday, his children decided to present their father with a unique gift. Rabbi Buxbaum heads Machon Yerushalayim, an institute which publishes *sefarim* by illustrious authors, including many great *Rashei Yeshivah*, and so the children had access to quite a number of

The Ways of the Righteous / 175

notables to assist them in carrying out their plan. The conspirators intended to mark the milestone with the presentation of a journal of birthday wishes from the prominent rabbis of the day. The leading letter, of course, was to be authored by the most prominent of them all: Reb Shlomo Zalman Auerbach.

When the Gaon was approached he readily agreed to participate. He wrote a very warm, full-length letter of good wishes and blessings for Reb Yosef, whom he held in high regard. His words of praise were effusive, and he was equally unstinting in his *berachos*.

Later that night, Rabbi Buxbaum's son was surprised to receive a phone call from Reb Shlomo Zalman. The Gaon had called to inquire if the letter was to the children's satisfaction. He said he had been a bit pressed for time when he had penned it, and wondered if they perhaps would like him to write a different one.

Likewise, when Reb Avigdor Nebanzahl published *B'Yitzchak Yikare* in tribute to his father's seventieth birthday, Reb Shlomo Zalman was asked to write an approbation in honor of the occasion. Reb Avigdor's son, Akiva, the ostensible courier, ended up serving as consultant and adviser for the Gaon, who sought his counsel on every line of the approbation.

❧ ❧ ❧

Years ago, a young *avrech* was sent to Reb Shlomo Zalman to obtain his signature on an appeal for *tzedakah* to finance an operation abroad for a child whose life was in danger. After inquiring about the case, Reb Shlomo Zalman agreed to sign, and the young man immediately rose and left.

When the *avrech* was halfway down the stairs, Reb Shlomo Zalman called him back. "*Chazal* tell us," he said, " 'Decorate yourself before decorating others.' " How can I advise others to contribute to a matter of *piku'ach nefesh* — of life and death — if I do not first contribute myself?" He handed the young man a handsome sum of money and asked him to give it to the needy family. "*Now*," he said, "you can publicize the appeal with my signature on it."

❧ ❧ ❧

A family included a jar of homemade jam in their Purim package of *mishlo'ach manos* to the Auerbachs. A few weeks later, the head of that family went to Reb Shlomo Zalman to ask him a halachic question. The moment he approached the Rav, Reb Shlomo Zalman greeted him warmly and said, "Please tell your wife that we eat her jam every morning and we find it very, very tasty."

The man was amazed. Hundreds of people — students at Kol Torah, present and former; members of the community; colleagues; and Jews from every walk of life who revered the Gaon, must have sent *mishlo'ach manos* on Purim to the Auerbachs. How could Reb Shlomo Zalman have distinguished from which package the jam he enjoyed had emerged, and furthermore, recalled several weeks later the identity of the sender?

Rabbi Michael Schoen, who was Reb Shlomo Zalman's regular driver once a week, received similar attention. After the passing of Rabbi Schoen's mother, who should show up at the memorial services but Reb Shlomo Zalman Auerbach. He sat through the entire evening of eulogies delivered in English, not comprehending a word, but nodding his head empathetically at all that was said, displaying respect and admiration for the deceased — a woman he had never even met.

❊ ❊ ❊

As an expression of his appreciation for the young man who used to escort Reb Shlomo Zalman, the Gaon never missed attending any of the fellow's family celebrations. Of course it was the young man's greatest pleasure to escort Reb Shlomo Zalman, but the Rav was so endowed with the attribute of gratitude that he wanted to demonstrate his gratefulness at every opportunity presented.

❊ ❊ ❊

Just outside the Yeshiva building, Reb Shlomo Zalman once encountered a peddler selling yarmulkes, pairs of *tzitzis*, and the like. The display of wares reminded him that he needed a new yarmulke, so he stepped up to the peddler and asked him if he carried the large square ones of the type he customarily wore. The peddler replied that he had none like that.

Reb Shlomo Zalman was about to walk away when it occurred to him that the man must feel bad, as he had already anticipated making a sale. For this reason Reb Shlomo Zalman purchased a new pair of *tzitzis*, although he really didn't need one.

The caretaker of the *mikveh* in Shaarei Chesed relates that once Reb Shlomo Zalman asked him if he needed some help. His reply was a firm "No." This was rather fortuitous, for had he given even the slightest indication of actually requiring assistance, chances are that Rabbi Auerbach would have rolled up his sleeves and helped him clean out the *mikveh*...

❋ ❋ ❋

A *ba'al teshuvah* who had never consulted Reb Shlomo Zalman before, came one day to see the Rav on a health-related matter. It seems the young man suffered from a particular illness and an important specialist in that field was visiting in Israel at the time. The young man asked the Rav if he should attempt to secure an appointment with the specialist. Reb Shlomo Zalman told the young man that indeed he should make every effort to see this physician and obtain his expert opinion.

Half an hour later the young man received a call from Reb Shlomo Zalman. The Rav had located the doctor, and was calling to give the young man the phone number!

A young rabbi once brought his unmarried older sister to Reb Shlomo Zalman for a blessing.

At the same time, he asked the Rav to have a talk with the woman. Reb Shlomo Zalman, immediately assessing the situation, gave the woman his blessing and then spoke with her at length, advising her not to be overly selective. As the rabbi and his sister were leaving, Reb Shlomo Zalman asked their last name.

The next day the woman received a call from a marriage broker who had a possible match to suggest. Apparently the Rav had not only made the referral to the marriage broker, but, with only the woman's last name to go on, had gone to the effort of finding out her telephone number as well.

❊ ❊ ❊

The Talmud teaches that a poor man can never claim that he is absolved from Torah study, for no one was as poor as Hillel, who learned diligently despite his poverty. Likewise a rich man can never claim that he is so busy managing his business that he is absolved from learning, for no one was as rich as Rabbi Eliezer, who learned Torah diligently. The example of Hillel מחייב את העניים — obliges the poor [to learn], while Eliezer ben Charsom מחייב את העשירים — obliges the rich [to learn]. The example of Reb Shlomo Zalman obliges those who have no time, for no one is as busy as he was, yet he found time for learning and for everything and everyone.

Whenever he attended a bris which was held in a hospital, he would be sure to inquire if there was anyone hospitalized there who was acquainted with him and would be pleased to have a visit from him. He was able to find so much time for such activities because he was an expert at utilizing every second of the day to the fullest. Efficiency experts would call that "maximizing one's time."

Reb Shlomo Zalman's door was open to everyone, and it was, literally, opened by the Gaon himself. He saw nothing inappropriate in a *Gadol* opening his front door to whosoever knocked. Among the thousands who came to him were also untold numbers of nudniks, *dreikups*, and other time-wasters who pestered him with every silliness dreamed up in the Middle East or abroad. Nonetheless, he would afford each and every one his patient attention, as if they were consulting him about the most earth-shattering matter.

Once some neighbors approached him about forming an ad hoc committee to pressure the municipality into installing road bumps on their street in order to slow down the through-traffic. The scene was almost comical: They presented their case to him as though he were a city official, quoting statistics real and imagined about the effectiveness of road bumps in curbing traffic accidents. They cited various data they had gleaned from their research, apparently forgetting that Reb Shlomo Zalman was just a neighbor, and incidentally a *Posek*. Still, he listened to them as patiently as he would have if they had been relating to him monumental *chiddushei Torah*, and needless to say, as the subject was a life-and-death issue, the Gaon treated it with appropriate seriousness.

His patience extended everywhere. If a child wished to photograph him, a family member would usually try to get the pesky youngster to disappear. Reb Shlomo Zalman, however, reacted quite differently. "What does it bother you?" he would say. "The child enjoys this and it's perfectly harmless, so let him shoot."

Once he was seen with a child sitting on his lap. This was not in and of itself an unusual occurrence, except that in this instance the child was not related to him. In fact, the boy seemed to be a complete stranger. At the Rav's side was another youngster, also not related to the Auerbachs in any way, and yet a third child was capturing this scene on film for posterity.

When asked what was going on, Reb Shlomo Zalman explained that the children had been trying to take a picture of him but had not been successful. He decided to help them out and make it a little easier for them by holding one of the three on his lap. This pose had to be rephotographed three separate times, as each child wanted a turn at sitting on the Gaon's lap.

Everyone seemed to want a picture of Reb Shlomo Zalman, which at times tried his patience. One evening some American students who had come to Shaarei Chesed to hear a talk from the Gaon's brother-in-law, Rabbi Shalom Schwadron, caught sight of Reb Shlom Zalman and quickly seized the moment. With flashes going off in dizzying abandon, Rabbi Shlomo Zalman found himself in the middle of a serious photo op — much to his disapproval. Reb Avigdor Nebanzahl, who was accompanying his Rav, managed to dispel the tension with an anecdote. He asked the Gaon, "What is the first question an American student will ask at the time of the advent of the Messiah?" and then answered the riddle himself: 'May I take a picture?' " The Gaon chuckled and continued on his way.

❃ ❃ ❃

Each time Reb Michel Gutfarb returned to Israel after undergoing medical treatment abroad, Reb Shlomo Zalman went to visit him at home. Once, Reb Michel was anxious to mark the occasion with a photograph. His wife, lifting the camera to her eyes, requested the Rav's permission, and Reb Shlomo Zalman readily agreed.

As Mrs. Gutfarb steadied the camera, she signaled for her husband to move out of the frame, but he misunderstood and instead of moving *out* he moved further *in* and joined Reb Shlomo Zalman in posing for the picture.

The cries of consternation that ensued elicited a dismissive wave of the hand from the Rav. He sensed that Mrs. Gutfarb hesitated to ask for a second snapshot, this time without her husband. Reb Shlomo Zalman turned to Reb Michel, whose visage bore the distressing effects of his medical treatments, and asked kindly, "What do you need a picture of yourself like this for?"

One day there was a knock on the door of the "hidden room" where Reb Shlomo Zalman learned in privacy wearing *tallis* and *tefillin*. The Rav always sequestered himself when clad in *tallis* and *tefillin* for fear that to appear in public this way would seem haughty. He opened the door to a rather startled, simple workman who was wearing only shorts and a T-shirt. Upon seeing the Rabbi attired in the most royal of Jewish raiment, his prayer shawl flowing from his shoulders like a king's robe and his *tefillin* like a crown on his head, the workman felt ashamed of his own appearance.

The man's face reddened beneath the stubble on his cheeks and he began to back away, excusing himself and mumbling that he had to go and get dressed. But Reb Shlomo Zalman stopped him with a smile and assured the hapless visitor that there was nothing wrong with his attire. "Working out in the sun I'm sure you must dress this way for your health."

On his way home from shul one brisk morning, Reb Shlomo Zalman encountered a jogger clad in "sweats" and running shoes, pounding the pavement of Shaarei Chesed, a sheen of perspiration glistening on his face in the Jerusalem sunlight. The face belonged to none other than Rabbi Berel Wein, who, when not engaged in spiritual guidance or the myriad educational and literary activities that occupy his time, relaxes at his Jerusalem retreat.

Rabbi Wein, abashed at meeting the Gaon in his somewhat unusual attire, silently hoped to retain his anonymity, but he of course greeted the Rav with appropriate deference. Reb Shlomo Zalman, however, was not deceived by the good Rabbi's disguise. He returned his neighbor's greeting and dismissed his embarrassment with a grin. "Nu,nu," he remarked, "one's health is also important!"

An Expert Opinion

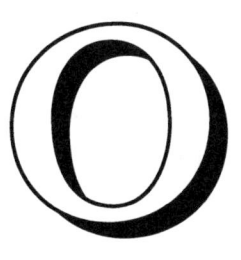NCE THERE WAS an opportunity for someone to give a one-time *shiur* at the Yeshiva, and the question arose as to who should deliver it and on which subject it should be given. Reb Shlomo Zalman volunteered his services, adding that he was prepared to deliver a *shiur* on any subject from the Tractates of *Berachos* through *Uktzin* — provided his audience was prepared to listen. Reb Shlomo Zalman's honest assertion revealed that not

only did he know the entire Talmud but he was capable of giving an in-depth *shiur* on any subject therein.

Although he had mastered the entire Torah, there were several areas in which Reb Shlomo Zalman excelled. In the realm of *Zera'im*, Reb Shlomo Zalman had no peer, as is attested to by his work *Ma'adanei Eretz*. Indeed, the Steipler wrote that it was impossible to learn *Zera'im* without the aid of this *sefer*. "It is a gift from Heaven," he said. "No one who begins to study it can put it down."

Even before he began teaching at Kol Torah, Reb Shlomo Zalman wrote *Ma'adanei Eretz*, on the Laws of *Shevi'is* and *Terumos* according to the order of the Rambam. In it he mentioned that he also had material to publish on the fifth chapter of *Terumos*. He did not explain, however, why this volume did not include his comments on that chapter, only that it had been his desire to publish his comments on the first five chapters of *Hilchos Terumos* together, as he felt that those chapters contained the foundations of all the מצוות התלויות בארץ — commandments that are contingent upon the Land of Israel.

Many years later he related that precisely at the time he was about to complete his work on the fifth chapter, he was invited to join the staff of Kol Torah. "I was not certain how to proceed. On the one hand, I wanted to complete my book; on the other hand, they were asking me to teach at the Yeshiva. I consulted my teacher, Reb Isser Zalman Meltzer, and he told me that teaching in the Yeshiva took precedence. So I stopped work on my book and went to the Yeshiva, hoping that with God's help I would find the time to complete the fifth chapter. But you know how it is. When you teach, you have the students to worry about, and the yeshiva as a whole. I never did find the time, and now I no longer have the strength to complete the fifth chapter."

When asked if he had ever considered retiring from education, the Rav replied that teaching Torah takes priority over everything else, even if one can accomplish three times as much without the burden of teaching.

When *ramim* from a particular yeshiva complained to Reb Shlomo Zalman that their salaries were extremely low, he answered that for the privilege of teaching Torah, the educators ought to pay the yeshiva, and that it is only out of necessity that a yeshiva supports its *ramim* so that they can spend their time engaged in Torah.

Reb Shlomo Zalman considered his teaching so important that in his will he left instructions to inscribe upon his headstone only these words: — העמיד תלמידים בישיבת קול תורה והרביץ תורה לרבים "He nurtured students at the Kol Torah Yeshiva and taught Torah to the masses."

One day a student at Kol Torah was seen slouching in a particularly unbecoming position, practically prone, as he took a written exam. Reb Shlomo Zalman approached him and said, "Actually we ought to study Torah standing in fear and trembling in awe. Unfortunately, we are weak, and so we sit. But to lie down...?!"

When Reb Shlomo Zalman made up his mind, nothing could sway him from what he believed to be the *emmes*. This did not mean that he always allowed his opinion to be known, or that he would publicize his ruling if it contradicted the view of a highly regarded rabbinic authority.

When a census was conducted several years ago in Israel, the Steipler ruled that it was forbidden to participate in it, for to do so violated the Torah precept which prohibited the counting of Jews. Whoever asked Reb Shlomo Zalman his opinion (myself included) did not receive an answer. It was readily apparent that Reb Shlomo Zalman disagreed with the Steipler's ruling, but he would not refute the Steipler or allow himself to be quoted on the matter. There were many such instances.

At one time certain Torah scholars issued a ruling that contradicted one of the Rav's halachic rulings. They then reported to the Steipler that there was a Rav in Jerusalem who ruled in a way which they found to be incorrect, certain that the Steipler would join them in deciding against the *psak* of Reb Shlomo Zalman. But this was not to be.

The Steipler became enraged at the audacity of those who had come to see him. "Reb Shlomo Zalman sits in Jerusalem," he roared at them, "and on his right rests the Divine Presence at the gate of Heaven, and on his left is the holy Torah. Against such a Jew you have the gall to open your mouths!"

Once Rabbi Yosef Buxbaum traveled to America with the newly appointed Rav of Jerusalem, Rabbi Yitzchak Kolitz. They were privileged to have an audience with the world-renowned *Gadol*, Reb Moshe Feinstein.

At first the three exchanged formalities and pleasantries until Rabbi Buxbaum related that he was on a mission from his Rav, Reb Shlomo Zalman Auerbach. As soon as Reb Moshe heard Reb Shlomo Zalman's name, his entire disposition altered. The *Gadol* focused his complete attention on what his guests had to say.

At the time, a controversial ruling of Reb Moshe's, written for the HATZOLOH ambulance corps, had been published. According to Rabbi Feinstein's *psak*, emergency medical personnel on call are permitted to travel back home on Shabbos from the scene of the emergency. Rabbi Buxbaum reported that Reb Shlomo Zalman disagreed with Reb Moshe's *psak* and wished to publish his own ruling on the matter, but not before first acquiring Reb Moshe's permission to do so.

Reb Moshe, clearly delighted over receiving regards from the great Israeli halachic authority, smiled his warm smile and happily awarded his consent. He then went on to speak a little about Reb Shlomo Zalman, as he had two of the Israeli Gaon's close *talmidim* in his house. Among the accolades he offered was: "People refer to Reb Shlomo Zalman as one of the greatest *rabbanim* in Yerushalayim, but I believe that he is truly the best in all of Eretz Yisrael!"

Reb Shlomo Zalman's request from Reb Moshe is a historic anomaly. It is unheard of for a Rav to request the permission of a colleague to print a responsum which disputes the colleague's position.

It was a great source of *kavod* to Reb Shlomo Zalman, and something that he genuinely cherished, when Reb Moshe telephoned him from time to time. Reb Shlomo Zalman's respect for Reb Moshe was such that he held him to be the *Rashkebehag* — the Rav of all Diaspora Jewry, and even entertained the thought that it was appropriate for everyone to tear *kriah* at the passing of this great sage.

Rabbi Yisrael Meir Lau, the current Chief Rabbi of Israel, was a disciple of Reb Shlomo Zalman and he would meticulously transcribe his master's classes. On occasion, Reb Shlomo Zalman would inspect Rabbi Lau's notebooks, and he once discovered a passage that truly upset him. Rabbi Lau had written in his notes that Reb Shlomo Zalman disputed what the Chazon Ish had said on a particular matter. "You may not say or even imply such a thing," Reb Shlomo Zalman chastised his disciple. "At most, you may write that I, perhaps, **understood** the matter a little differently..."

Another instance in which Reb Shlomo Zalman "understood the matter a little differently" from the Chazon Ish was in an aspect of the use of electricity on Shabbos. In 5695 (1935), Reb Shlomo Zalman published his *Me'orei Esh*. At the time, he wished to publish a thorough discussion of his halachic opinion that opening an electric circuit does not constitute *binyan,* one of the halachic categories of forbidden labor on Shabbos. However, a number of highly regarded authorities assured him that no one would ever even consider such a possibility. Reb Shlomo Zalman decided not to publish his excursus.

Some ten years later, the Chazon Ish published a work on *hilchos Shabbos* in which he asserted that opening an electric circuit on Shabbos does constitute *binyan*. Reb Shlomo Zalman always regretted not having published his discussion of the topic, but the idea of publishing a contradiction of the Chazon Ish's ruling was unthinkable for him.

Reb Shlomo Zalman did permit his correspondence with the Chazon Ish to be published, however, and it is apparent from these letters that he did not concur with the opinion of the Chazon Ish.

The Traits of a Tzaddik

EB SHLOMO ZALMAN, in his earlier years, enjoyed a warm relationship with Rabbi Avraham Yitzchak Kook, the first chief Rabbi of Israel. He would visit with him, observe his actions, and learn from him. Their relationship was so close, in fact, that Rav Kook officiated at Reb Shlomo Zalman's wedding.

Even though many *Gedolim* voiced strong reservations concerning Rav Kook's apparent overtolerance of nationalistic Zionist causes and individuals, Reb Shlomo Zalman never ceased to speak of him with the very highest admiration.

Reb Shlomo Zalman's classic work *Me'orei Esh* contains approbations from Rav Abba Yaakov Hakohen Borochov, Rav Isser Zalman Meltzer, and Rav Avraham Yitzchak Kook. The approbation which appears first is that of Rav Kook. Several years ago when this *sefer* was reprinted, some individuals pressed Reb Shlomo Zalman to omit Rav Kook's approbation. The Gaon was equally emphatic in his response: "If Rav Kook's approbation does not appear, then none of them will appear!"

Considering Reb Shlomo Zalman's aversion to matters of a political nature, it was startlingly unusual when he intervened in the internal affairs of a particular organization. Needless to say, the Gaon's advice was always sought and welcomed, but in the area of organization politics, no one had ever succeeded in eliciting his response in the past.

The issue at hand was whether to accept a certain candidate for a key position in this Torah organization. Reb Shlomo Zalman had recommended *not* to accept the nominee. His unprecedented intervention was triggered by the fact that the candidate in question always referred to Rav Kook as simply "Kook". Such a flippant dismissal of a great man by someone of significantly lesser status was sufficient grounds for disqualification by Reb Shlomo Zalman's standards.

Once, the Gaon was riding in a taxi with one of the *rabbanim* from Kol Torah. His companion began to relate that he had found the explanation of a complex subject under examination at the yeshiva, in a particular book. But when he mentioned the name of the *sefer*, Reb Shlomo Zalman stopped him and refused to hear the explanation, saying that the book contained denigrating remarks about Rav Kook.

Reb Shlomo Zalman's respect for Rav Kook was evident from the numerous stories he would tell which highlighted the brilliant and charismatic attributes of the Chief Rabbi.

One of these stories involved Reb Aryeh Levine, the "*tzaddik* of Jerusalem." One day, Rav Kook had ordered a car to transport him to some important function, and in those days the very presence of a car on the streets of Jerusalem was an unrivaled spectacle. Automobiles were at a premium in Palestine at the time, and once a driver arrived, one never kept him waiting.

Just as the car pulled up at the Chief Rabbi's house, Reb Aryeh Levine made a simultaneous appearance. Rav Kook already had one foot out the door, but as soon as Reb Aryeh Levine explained that he needed Rav Kook's assistance in a philanthropic matter, the Chief Rabbi did an about-face. He ushered his guest into his house, removed the *spuddik* that graced his head, and took off his long coat. Then the two began to compose a letter to help Reb Aryeh raise funds for a worthy cause.

Reb Shlomo Zalman was witness to this scene and it made a profound and lasting impression upon him.

❋ ❋ ❋

Reb Shlomo Zalman related that there was once a *Gadol* in Jerusalem, a great zealot who despised Rav Kook. The scholar's feelings were so intense that he frequently voiced vitriolic, disparaging remarks about the Chief Rabbi.

One Friday afternoon, this zealot was passing Rav Kook's home, when he heard a most moving recitation of *Shir Ha-Shirim*. He looked up and saw that the voice he had heard was none other than Rav Kook's. The glowing, angelic expression on his face as he chanted the "holiest of writings" affected the zealot so profoundly that he was sure he was beholding a visage of the Divine Presence itself. At that moment this *Gadol* pledged never to besmirch Rav Kook again.

Reb Shlomo Zalman and Reb Aryeh Levine were dear friends. Those who were very close to Reb Shlomo Zalman believe they detected in the Gaon's behavior conduct that equaled, if not excelled, the kind of righteous kindness for which Reb Aryeh, the man whom Reb Shlomo Zalman so admired, was famous.

Reb Shlomo Zalman had an abiding affection for the settlements and their settlers, which was expressed not in mere words but in concrete gestures. In his capacity as head of the presidium of the Committee for Family Purity in Israel, he would personally visit the new *mikva'os* that were built in Judea and Samaria.

He also made a point of including in his annual visit to *Me'aras Ha-Machpelah* between Rosh Hashanah and Yom Kippur, a tour of the Jewish enclaves in Hebron. After praying at the Cave of the Patriarchs, he would stop at the Avraham *Avinu* Synagogue, Beit Hadassah, Beit Romano, and the old Hebron cemetery, where many great *tzaddikim* are buried. His presence gave much-needed encouragement to the idealistic families who have re-established a Jewish presence in the holy city where their predecessors had been massacred in the 1929 Arab riots.

At one visit to Tel Rumeida, Reb Shlomo Zalman noted the appallingly cramped living conditions. The settlers' caravans were situated almost one on top of the other, as the government had refused to allocate any more space for living quarters at that site. Reb Shlomo Zalman empathized with the families' plight and blessed them with all the best and more spacious accommodations. Three days later, the government granted permission for the settlers to add one more room to each existing caravan.

The Rav's position on the settlements may, perhaps, be deduced from a brief Torah thought he would relate on Sukkos: There are two mitzvas that involve a person's entire body, he would say, and they are the mitzva of *sukkah* and the mitzva of *Yishuv Eretz Yisrael* — living in the Land of Israel. Just as the Law regarding the *sukkah* is תעשה ולא מן העשוי, i.e., that for the thatch to be kosher it must be *ta'aseh*, something that is made afresh, and not *assui*, something that already existed, so should the Law be regarding the settlement of Eretz Yisrael.

During one year's visit to *Me'aras Ha-Machpelah*, a guide pointed out that they were entering the chamber of *Yeshenei Chevron* — those who sleep [are in their final resting place] in Hebron, i.e., Adam and Chavah, Avraham and Sarah, Yitzchak and Rivkah, and Yaakov and Leah. As soon as the Gaon heard the name of the room he halted and cried out in a shrill voice, "*Uru, uru, yeshenei Chevron!*" — "Awake, awake you slumberers of Hebron!" His spontaneous outpouring of emotion charged passions all around.

On matters of politics Reb Shlomo Zalman would never allow himself to be quoted, yet it was no secret that his sentiments were not with the Leftists. He deplored the policies of the Rabin/Peres government which came to power towards the end of his life, and claimed that he had had no fear of SCUDS from Iraq, but was terribly frightened of SCUDS that could emanate from Oslo.

Understandably, Reb Shlomo Zalman had no great respect for politicians; however, he felt that Menachem Begin had been somewhat "cleaner" than the rest. This unusual and atypical comment was prompted by former Prime Minister Begin's state of depression after his wife's passing, a depression so profound that it affected his ability to continue functioning. Other politicians, the Rav noted, seemed to adjust quickly to the death of a loved one and to get on with their lives as though nothing had happened.

❇ ❇ ❇

Reb Shlomo Zalman abhorred conflicts and controversy. He often said that he harbored resentment towards no man. For him, conflict was the very worst of all evils, and thus avoiding conflict was a matter of life and death. He once remarked in disbelief that some people seemed so eager to achieve a particular goal that they were even willing to enter into disputes in order to achieve it, but "I prefer to concede on almost anything to avoid a *machlokes*. When I read any sort of criticism," he added, "I always look to see if the writer first praises the work and its author and then comments on or criticizes a specific aspect or detail. If he does, I know that the criticism is genuine and therefore permissible. But if the piece *opens* with criticism and attacks the author or his book, then it is sheer *machlokes* and thus forbidden. Only when a person knows the value and importance of his fellow man can he criticize him without descending to controversy."

Someone once visited Reb Shlomo Zalman and overheard (as did anyone else in a five-block radius) two people engaged in a very heated and acrimonious dispute. They had obviously come to the Rav for a ruling but not before each had vented his side of the argument. Even in the presence of the Gaon they were unable to restrain themselves from shouting, so high did their emotions run on this issue.

When the two had exhausted themselves, they turned to Reb Shlomo Zalman for his opinion, but to their amazement they received far more than they had bargained for. In moments, not only had the Gaon rendered his decision, but he also had settled the dispute to the mutual satisfaction of both parties. The witness to this event was astonished to see that the gentlemen who had so recently almost come to blows, left Reb Shlomo Zalman's home in an elated mood of camaraderie.

❃ ❃ ❃

Before the most recent Israeli national elections there was enormous pressure upon Reb Shlomo Zalman to express support for the *Degel Ha-Torah* party. Indeed, Rav Eliezer Shach and Rav Yosef Shalom Elyashiv brought their own influence to bear upon him to come out and support the party endorsed by many *Rashei Yeshivah*.

Reb Shlomo Zalman, however, refused to veer from his path of non-involvement. Nothing could impel him to get embroiled in the fierce debate between Degel and Agudah, and in the end the Degel supporters said, "If you won't endorse us, then at least support Agudah — one way or another, you must take a stand!"

But this too was to no avail. He refused to become entangled in a political issue for he feared that such involvement would disqualify him in certain quarters as an *Ish Ha-Halachah* — the title given to Reb Chaim Brisker, which he liked the most. Ultimately, Reb Shlomo Zalman earned enormous respect for dissociating himself from both the national and the municipal elections.

In the midst of the election campaign, the Rav paid a condolence call on a mourner from a very distinguished Sephardic family. No sooner had he entered than the bereaved family began to extol Reb Shlomo Zalman's behavior and sing his praises for having refused to be drawn into the political morass, and they expressed regret that others had not had this perspicacity.

Reb Shlomo Zalman surprised them with his reaction. Far from graciously accepting the compliment, he quickly straightened out the family, saying: "You should be aware that the individuals in the news are Jewish public officials, honestly and faithfully serving their people. These individuals are no less than the representatives of some of the finest *Gedolim* of this generation. I strongly recommend that you curb your criticism."

The mourners immediately begged forgiveness.

❈ ❈ ❈

It was Reb Shlomo Zalman's unswerving policy not to issue approbations for *sefarim*. When I asked him more than a decade ago for an approbation for my first book (featured on the opening page of this volume), he told me, "It has already been ten years since I have given anyone an approbation. I have lost my best friends over this issue," he confessed. That the Gaon ultimately was gracious enough to award me his *haskamah* (and such a warm and enthusiastic one) is a gesture that I shall cherish all my life.

Because of something that once happened, which he revealed to no one, Reb Shlomo Zalman adopted his policy of not issuing *haskamos*. An author once asked him for an approbation and the Rav, in line with his standard policy, declined. The fellow who had introduced the author to Reb Shlomo Zalman explained to the Rav that there was a *shalom bayis* issue at stake which could be resolved if an approbation were to be issued. In no time the authors request was fulfilled.

Reb Shlomo Zalman once asked Rabbi Meir Schlesinger, who was *Rosh Yeshivah* at Yeshivas Sha'alvim, to consider accepting a particular Kol Torah student. The boy, it seemed, was not cut out for Kol Torah and Reb Shlomo Zalman had hoped that the enviroment at Sha'alvim might suit him and enable him to adjust better. Rabbi Schlesinger heeded his mentor's advice and gave the student an interview and an oral exam. However, it was patently obvious from the exam results that this boy was not cut out for Sha'alvim either, and he was not accepted.

A little while later, a senior member of the Kol Torah faculty approached Rabbi Schlesinger demanding to know how he had had the audacity to insult Reb Shlomo Zalman. "The *Rosh Yeshivah* asks you to accept a student, and you decide to go and test him?!"

Rabbi Schlesinger felt he had indeed been remiss in ignoring his Rav's instructions and immediately went to apologize.

"I have come to beg your forgiveness...," Rabbi Schlesinger began.

"Forgiven," Reb Shlomo Zalman cut him off. "Now tell me what it's about."

Rabbi Schlesinger related his story, to which the Gaon reacted by saying, "Now you must *truly* beg my forgiveness! To think that I would expect you to accept a student without testing him, just because I said so, means that your opinion of me is terribly low. And for that, you really do need to apologize!"

❊ ❊ ❊

In his last will, Rabbi Yehudah He-Chasid wrote that he forbade any sons born to his family in that generation to be named either Yehudah or Shmuel, that is, either his or his father's name. Reb Shlomo Zalman suggested that the explanation for this request may be the not-infrequent arguments among young couples over which name to give their child, the father wishing to name the baby after his side of the family; the mother wishing to name the baby after her side of the family.

Rabbi Yehudah He-Chasid, realizing that the desire to honor one's parents might lead, God forbid, to strife and argument, had found a formula for avoiding potential problems.

Reb Shlomo Zalman hastened to point out that this lesson — of seeking ways to avoid potential arguments — was applicable to *all* generations.

Musar, or ethical teachings, is an essential element in yeshiva curricula, and works of this nature are usually studied at the end of the daily learning session or before prayer services. Reb Shlomo Zalman, however, was occasionally seen perusing a volume of ethics in the morning, before leaving for yeshiva.

When asked why he chose this unusual hour for *musar* study, the Rav explained that often after delivering the Gemara lesson at yeshiva, students would bombard him with infuriatingly foolish questions. By studying the ethical teachings in advance he was able to fortify himself and thereby avoid losing his patience with the boys.

❈ ❈ ❈

Reb Shlomo Zalman would go to great lengths to avoid arguments and promote *shalom*. Once he disappeared for three hours and no one knew his whereabouts until it was revealed that he had gone to a distant neighborhood to convince a woman not to get divorced. On another occasion, he devoted a great deal of time to explaining to a woman that what she viewed as anguish and frustration was really a blessing in disguise.

This particular woman and her husband were experiencing inordinate hardships in finding a suitable match for each of their children. As one after another of the children grew past their prime in terms of marriageability, the parents' anguish intensified. Finally, one of them became engaged — the youngest daughter.

The mother found this twist of fate — the youngest finding a match before any of her older siblings — a little hard to bear. Aside from deviating from long-held family traditions, her daughter's engagement seemed to indicate a sealing of fate for the other children.

Reb Shlomo Zalman had put the woman at ease by relating the following anecdote:

If a family loses the key to their house and are locked outside, the only way to open the door without smashing it is from within. How can this be accomplished? By squeezing the youngest child through an open window to turn the key and let the others in.

"Perhaps," Reb Shlomo Zalman had suggested with a twinkle in his eye, "it is the youngest one who has the key for all of the rest..."

❉ ❉ ❉

Apparently Reb Shlomo Zalman was not from the contemporary school of psychologists which believes one must always speak and reveal whatever is on his mind, as the following story demonstrates.

Reb Michel Gutfarb's unfortunate medical dilemmas are common knowledge, hence his name is on the lips and in the prayers of countless Jews throughout the world. Sadly, such problems have not been restricted to him alone.

Recently, his wife Naomi was diagnosed as having a life-threatening medical problem that required urgent treatment.

Mrs. Gutfarb was very taken by the professionalism, thoroughness and courteous bedside manner of the local *kupat cholim* (health fund) doctor who examined her. As treatment for the disease required significant medical intervention, Mrs. Gutfarb was eager that this doctor be the one to administer it.

Reb Michel, however, felt that therapy of this magnitude required the supervision of a far more senior physician with an international reputation. As with all matters of consequence in the Gutfarb family, Reb Shlomo Zalman was consulted.

The Gutfarbs arrived at the Gaon's house late at night on the Thursday prior to Reb Shlomo Zalman's admission to the hospital (eleven days before his passing). The Rav listened to their problem and then replied unequivocally with this quote: איזוהי אשה כשרה? כל שעושה רצון בעלה — "Who is a proper wife? She who fulfills her husbands desires," concurring with Reb Michel's insistence that such a procedure required the supervision of a world-class specialist.

Reb Shlomo Zalman advised the couple to immediately go and consult with Rabbi Benny Fisher, an expert in recommending and referring people to the appropriate doctor to treat complicated medical cases. Rabbi Fisher was a student of Reb Shlomo Zalman's whom the Gaon had helped to enter this field. Even before the Gutfarbs arrived, Rabbi Fisher had already received a call from Reb Shlomo Zalman to apprise him of the situation.

Mrs. Gutfarb recalls having felt slighted when she and her husband left Reb Shlomo Zalman's home, by the fact that the Gaon had not asked for her full name so that he could include her in his prayers. It seemed to be such an egregious error of omission and a deviation from customary procedure, certainly from the kind of conduct the Gutfarbs had grown accustomed to seeing around Reb Shlomo Zalman, that they could not help but notice.

Reasoning that since of late the welfare of all of *Klal Yisrael* had been resting solely the Rav's broad shoulders, Mrs. Gutfarb thought it was perhaps too much for Reb Shlomo Zalman to accept yet another burden upon himself. Although the rationalization rang true, in her heart of hearts she still felt some hurt, especially as she knew how devotedly Reb Shlomo Zalman prayed on behalf of her husband: The Gaon had once confessed that he prayed for Michel the exact same way that he prayed for himself.

Mrs. Gutfarb's surgery was scheduled for a Tuesday. The day before, Reb Michel went to visit Reb Shlomo Zalman to discuss other matters unrelated to his wife's condition. But as soon as Michel walked into the Auerbach home, Reb Shlomo Zalman demanded, "What is your wife's name? I intentionally did not ask when she was here so as not to frighten her or make her overly worried or concerned."

❀ ❀ ❀

The Traits of a Tzaddik / 215

The downtrodden who came to Reb Shlomo Zalman for a blessing would receive a standard reply: "The most important thing is to be happy. Then everything will work out."

To those who were ill and plagued with problems, Reb Shlomo Zalman never tired of offering encouragement. He always quoted the verse, "One who trusts in God will be surrounded by kindness," and he was also wont to quote the Gemara in *Bava Basra*: "He who does charity habitually will have sons who are wise, wealthy, and well versed in the Aggadah."

To those who were close to him who might complain about their health, he was not particularly sympathetic. "Have you ever heard me complain?" he would ask rhetorically.

❊ ❊ ❊

Reb Dovid Goldwicht was a key assistant in Reb Shlomo Zalman's philanthropic endeavors. The two sustained hundreds of families in sophisticated and enterprising ways. Many of their "customers" never knew they were receiving charity and several of them would never have accepted money had it ever been offered to them as a donation or a grant.

A great advantage of this *tzedakah* undertaking was that it had continued access to the phenomenal brain power of Reb Shlomo Zalman Auerbach. The very same brilliance and innovative thinking which made him into the Posek Ha-dor was harnassed for creatively providing for those who fervently wished *not* to be provided for, yet whose need was apparent all the same.

One such problematic candidate was a learned student who was unable to make ends meet but was too proud to accept charity. Reb Shlomo Zalman proposed the following scheme: He explained to the prospective recipient that the money in question was merely a loan and as documentary proof he produced a notebook entitled *L'k'she-yarchiv* — "For when the resources will expand." Then the Gaon worked out with the borrower an advantageous form of linking to the dollar the sums loaned in local currency, thereby furthering the illusion that this was indeed a legitimate business transaction.

Convinced, the *avrech* agreed to accept the loan at the favorable terms offered and never had the feeling, to the day of his death, that he had in fact accepted charity.

During one meeting with the Rav, Reb Dovid Goldwicht pointed out that the lot of a particular widow on their list had now improved and so she was no longer in need of charitable assistance. Reb Shlomo Zalman concurred with Reb Dovid's assessment, but felt that something should be given to her nonetheless. "Although she no longer needs the money, her spirits are always lifted by our regular visits. We must therefore continue the practice, under this pretext or another, of visiting her."

One Thursday evening Reb Dovid Goldwicht came to Reb Shlomo Zalman's home to discuss a particular *tzedakah* issue that required immediate attention. The two agreed to meet the next day at the Shaare Zedek Hospital at a specific hour to pursue the matter. His mission clear, Reb Dovid rose to depart, but Rebbetzin Auerbach suddenly began to bless Reb Dovid, declaiming a lengthy, well-thought-out benediction. Reb Shlomo Zalman looked at his Rebbetzin with incredulity and commented, "I never knew you were a Rebbe."

That very night the Rebbetzin took ill and Reb Shlomo Zalman escorted her to the hospital where he spent the entire night at her bedside. Two days later she would be summoned to the Heavenly Assembly.

On Friday morning Reb Shlomo Zalman sent word to Reb Dovid that there was no need for them to meet at the hospital as he had been there himself the previous night and had managed while there to take care of the matter they had discussed.

When Reb Dovid Goldwicht's health deteriorated, his family decided to assemble a minyan at once to recite the prayers involved in a *shinui ha-shem*. This special name-changing ritual, performed for one who is critically ill, has Kabbalistic origins and is a form of spiritual intervention in the Heavenly Court, a supplication for a reprieve or commutation of the apparent death sentence. On a simplistic level, the idea is to confound the Angel of Death by altering the patient's name and thereby invalidating the "summons" issued in his former name.

Representatives hurried to Reb Shlomo Zalman at midnight to inform him of their plan. When the Gaon asked where they hoped to find a quorum of ten Jews at that hour, as required for the name-changing procedure, they replied that they assumed they could find one at the Zichron Moshe neighborhood

The Traits of a Tzaddik / 219

shtiblach, a group of small shuls in a religious neigborhood noted for very late-hour services.

Reb Shlomo Zalman was doubtful. He said that while it was likely they would find a minyan there, it was unlikely they could assemble ten men who were willing to recite the entire lengthy procedure of *shinui ha-shem*, a not insignificant detail which they had overlooked.

The Gaon suggested that they go instead to the *Kosel*, where worshipers gathered at all hours of the day and night for the express purpose of praying. Those present at the Western Wall were therefore more likely to be amenable to joining in a *shinui ha-shem* service. "And," Reb Shlomo Zalman added, "you can count me in."

The Rav and several others from Shaarei Chesed made their way to the *Kosel*, where they succeeded in putting together a minyan. Some onlookers who noticed the renowned Reb Shlomo Zalman at that very late hour, concluded that the octagenarian *Gadol* must have some spare time and so, as soon as the prayers were completed, they clustered around him to ask some questions. It seemed they had been saving up their queries for just such an opportunity, but Reb Shlomo Zalman begged off, explaining that in fact he did not have any spare time. He had only interrupted his nocturnal learning schedule for this worthy cause.

Reb Shlomo Zalman was particular to perform the mitzva of visiting the sick at the very first opportunity, never delaying its performance to a more convenient time. The Rabbinic dictum, "Do not postpone a mitzva which falls into your hands" was one of his mottos. Every morning between nine o'clock — when he finished his breakfast — and ten o'clock — when he began learning — he managed to comfort two or three mourners, attend two to three circumcisions, and accomplish other sundry mitzvas, on a daily basis!

Once, as Reb Michel Gutfarb was driving Reb Shlomo Zalman home, a drunkard approached the car and loudly demanded a letter of recommendation endorsing him to collect charity.

Reb Shlomo Zalman referred him to Rabbi Rosenthal, the Rav of the neighborhood, and Reb Michel escorted the inebriated fellow to the Rabbi's house. A few minutes later, the drunkard stormed into the Auerbach home and repeated his demand for a letter from Reb Shlomo Zalman.

Reb Michel grabbed the man by his shirtfront and forcibly evicted him from the house. When he returned from this unpleasant task, he found an irate Reb Shlomo Zalman. "How dare you throw such a downtrodden soul out of my home!" the Rav reprimanded him.

Reb Michel was dumbstruck. The Gaon had never spoken this way to him before. He tried to defend his actions, claiming that he had feared the man was unstable and might have attacked the Rav.

Reb Shlomo Zalman was not impressed. "You don't have to worry about me," the venerable Gaon said dismissively. "I can take care of myself."

❈ ❈ ❈

As Reb Michel was very close to Reb Shlomo Zalman, some tried to exploit this relationship for their own ends. Authors seeking approbations, or administrators hoping for a letter from Reb Shlomo Zalman of support for their *kollel*, and many others, would first make their appeal to Reb Michel in the hope that he would act as a liaison.

However, if Reb Michel ever approached Reb Shlomo Zalman regarding an issue other than *tzedakah*, the area in which he so excelled and for which he was the Rav's active partner, Reb Shlomo Zalman would quickly admonish him to remain focused on his specialty and not dabble in unrelated matters.

Stringently Lenient

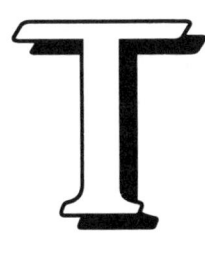ORAH IS IMMUTABLE. It was given to the Jewish People in its entirety at Mount Sinai and passed on intact from generation to generation, to the present day. But while the Torah — the body of Jewish Law consisting of the Written Law and the Oral Law — has remained unchanged over more than three millennia, circumstances have changed considerably since the days when our ancestors wandered in the wilderness. The challenge through the ages has been to apply Torah Law to the existing circumstances, keeping pace with the continuing technological and societal

developments, and this responsibility has fallen to our greatest Torah scholars, the *Gedolim* and *Poskim* — the halachic decisors of each generation.

In order to render a ruling or an opinion that is at once true to Torah Law and applicable to contemporary circumstances, a *Posek* must be a master of both. And in order to render a *lenient* ruling on a complex halachic subject, the decisor must have a phenomenal grasp of every nuance, must be utterly certain he is right, and must have the courage of his convictions to allow that opinion to be known. For if he erred in his understanding of the Law, he will cause others to transgress — a sin of the highest order.

Reb Shlomo Zalman was a *Posek* whose rulings affected the lives of every observant Jew. Rav Yehoshua Neuwirth's classic, *Shemiras Shabbos Kehilchasah*, is richly based on the rulings of Reb Shlomo Zalman. In the realm of technology, electronics, agriculture, and medicine most of the trailblazing halachic guidelines were interpreted by Reb Shlomo Zalman. In virtually every discipline and facet of the Law, he was a *machmir* when necessary and also a *mekel* — a halachic decisor who, wherever and whenever possible, interpreted

Stringently Lenient / 225

the Law from a lenient perspective. However, in his own personal practice he followed numerous stringencies, going beyond the letter of the Law and thereby enhancing his performance and observance of the mitzvahs.

The Israel Electric Company, which is staffed primarily by Jews, controls and provides electricity throughout the country. Thus the question arose as to the permissibility of deriving benefit on Shabbos from what may involve Jewish labor. Reb Shlomo Zalman was the most prominent halachic authority who ruled that it was indeed permissible to benefit from the Israel Electric Company, and whenever people asked him about his personal practice, he would reply, "I certainly use electricity on Shabbos." In essence, this statement was true: the Rav did in fact benefit from streetlights and other public facilities that used electricity, but within the walls of his own home a more stringent policy was observed. The Auerbach house was illuminated by gas lanterns and powered by batteries on Shabbos.

The Israeli banking system routinely allows depositors to overdraw their checking accounts, often by thousands of shekels, and then retroactively charges interest on the overdraft. Reb Shlomo Zalman tried to find a halachic basis for permitting this procedure but was never really satisfied with the standard *hetter iska* — a business agreement which allows the payment of pre-agreed, fixed, shared profits (adopted to preclude Torah-forbidden interest payments) — which most Israeli banks use regarding overdrafts. To circumvent this thorny issue, the Rav maintained both a checking account and a savings account and gave explicit instructions to the bank that if he should overdraw the checking account, the bank was to cover the deficit immediately from the savings account. This way he avoided paying interest.

Among Reb Shlomo Zalman's other personal stringencies was the donning of *tefillin* of Rabbenu Tam in the afternoons.*

Every morning Reb Shlomo Zalman would walk to shul via a relatively lengthy, circuitous route. Although a far more direct path existed, leading from his house right to the shul en-

---

* Rabbenu Tam, a grandson of Rashi, disagreed with his illustrious grandfather on the correct sequence of the Torah segments placed inside the *tefillin*. Rashi's opinion is the universally accepted one, but those individuals who wish to be absolutely certain they have fulfilled the mitzvah of donning *tefillin* may use Rashi's, followed by Rabbenu Tam's.

Stringently Lenient / 227

trance, he persisted in following his taxing roundabout pattern. There was much speculation on the subject since the direct footpath was indisputably on public property and his use of it would not have been an infringement of a private domain. It was a garden passage, adorned with flowers and maintained by the municipality; it was paved and terraced with steps for the convenience of all pedestrians. The Gaon's reasoning remained a mystery.

Only the closest "insiders" were privy to the Gaon's thoughts on the matter. He contended that although the garden clearly was public property, the houses that lined this particular garden happened to be on ground level, unlike most of the other homes in Shaarei Chesed, which were built above the street level or set back from the street, and he feared that walking on a path where one might inadvertently look into people's homes would lead to a היזק ראיה — damage caused by an invasion of privacy.

In addition, the Gaon was aware of the fact that the garden passage had not always been there. The municipality had decided one day to pave a path there, but had not first consulted the residents who would be affected by it. In all likelihood, they would not have been in favor of the idea. Reb Shlomo Zalman did not wish to walk on a road which was a source of annoyance or worse to those residents.

In his later years, Reb Shlomo Zalman was obliged to eat something prior to the morning prayer service. Before doing so, he would recite the verse from *Tehillim* 30:10: "What profit would my blood be, if I went down to the grave? Will the dust praise You? Will it declare your faithfulness?" When members of the family asked him why he chose to say this particular passage before eating, the Rav replied that the prohibition of eating before *Shacharis* is derived from *Vayikra* 19:26: "You shall not eat anything with the blood." The Gemara interprets this verse to mean: Do not eat until you have first prayed for your life. "Thus it is proper," Reb Shlomo Zalman explained, "that if I must eat before going to shul, I at least recite one verse which embodies a kind of prayer for my blood and my life."*

---

* This practice was earlier adopted by Rav Kook, who would recite the entire chapter of *Psalms*.

Rabbi Michael Schoen, who had the privilege of driving Reb Shlomo Zalman once a week, always used the opportunity to resolve complex questions that arose during his yeshiva lectures. He related that on one occasion the Rav's daughter joined them for the ride from Bayit Vegan. Quite naturally, when she got into the car she started a conversation with her father, but the Gaon quickly cut her off. "I am not on my own time now," he explained, "so I may not engage in personal conversation."

❈ ❈ ❈

The commonly used text for *Birkas Ha-Gomel* — the blessing of thanksgiving for being rescued from a perilous situation — is as follows: ברוך הגומל לחייבים טובות שגמלני כל טוב — "Blessed be You...Who bestows good things upon the undeserving, for bestowing every goodness upon me." Reb Shlomo Zalman believed that this standard text was imprecise and proposed it be emended.

His reasoning was that if someone fell out of a tree or was released from jail, if he crossed the desert unharmed, or escaped from a sinking ship, while it was true that the Almighty had saved his life, it was fair to assume that there were even *better* situations than the one to which he escaped. That is, what the Almighty bestowed upon him was indeed *good*, and for that the survivor should be duly grateful, but it was not the *best* possible situation or all the very best he might ever be awarded. Accordingly, Reb Shlomo Zalman's text omitted the word *kol* — "every." The respondents, however, should reply as they appropriately do in the standard version: "He Who bestowed a good thing upon you, may He bestow *every* goodness upon you, *always*."

The morning prayer, "These are the precepts whose fruits a person enjoys in this world but whose principal remains intact for him in the World to Come: honoring one's father and mother, acts of kindness...and the study of Torah is equivalent to them all," would get a special addendum from Reb Shlomo Zalman.

It was his custom — and one which he introduced to his family — to conclude this prayer with the words of the *Talmud Yerushalmi* in Tractate *Pe'ah*: "Four things will a man be punished for in this world and whose principal remains intact for him in the World to Come: idolatry, immorality...and the sin of slander is equivalent to all of the sins."

❋ ❋ ❋

A Yemenite student at the yeshiva asked Reb Shlomo Zalman to officiate at his wedding. Before the ceremony the Rav discovered that one of the designated witnesses was a member of an obscure sect of Jews whose members do not believe in the *Zohar Ha-Kadosh* and whose trustworthiness as a witness may therefore be suspect. The individual was himself a rabbi, so in order that no one be offended and that there be no possible question concerning the validity of the marriage, the Gaon announced that he himself would be a witness and the other rabbi would officiate as the *mesader kiddushin*. The rabbi, of course, wished to defer to the Gaon, but Reb Shlomo Zalman prevailed. There was no room for leniency in so vital a subject as *kiddushin*.

❋ ❋ ❋

Reb Shlomo Zalman's respect and deference for latter-day *Poskim* was absolute. The esteem and veneration in which he held the words of Rabbi Moshe Feinstein were legendary. Nevertheless, there were instances where he felt that either an earlier *Posek* was mistaken in his reasoning or the situation which obtained when that *Posek* had rendered his ruling differed significantly from today's circumstances. Reb Avigdor Nebanzahl, one of the Rav's closest disciples, relates that the Gaon once pointed out that something he was doing was not halachically correct. Reb Avigdor replied that he was acting in accordance with the *Mishnah Berurah*, the authoritative foundation for contemporary halachic decisions.

Reb Shlomo Zalman maintained that in this particular instance either the author of the *Mishnah Berurah*, the Chafetz Chayim — despite his undisputed greatness — was mistaken, or the circumstances had changed. The Gaon always stressed that it was essential to know the reason that the *Mishnah Berurah* (and others) had ruled the way they did. For example, there are clauses and sections within the *Mishnah Berurah* that were applicable to the geographic location of Radin, where the Chafetz Chayim lived, but are not necessarily applicable to that of Jerusalem, New York or London.

In Jerusalem (as in all cities that were walled in at the time of Joshua) Purim is celebrated on the fifteenth rather than the fourteenth of Adar, known as Shushan Purim.* There was, and remains, a significant polemic regarding the observance of Purim in the new neighborhoods of Jerusalem that are some distance from the Old City. The discussion revolves around whether these areas, which clearly were not included in the walled city of antiquity, should celebrate Purim or Shushan Purim.

Reb Shlomo Zalman cut through all the arguments and disputes, which had resulted in anomalies such as parts of certain neighborhoods celebrating on the fourteenth while across the street their neighbors waited for the fifteenth. He ruled that any area under the jurisdiction of the Jerusalem municipality was subject to the same law as the walled part of Jerusalem. His reasoning was that it was illogical and lacked halachic foundation to subdivide the city when all the residents have accepted upon themselves the authority of the

---

* The only walled city which *definitely* celebrates Purim on the fifteenth is Jerusalem. Other ancient walled cities which read the Megillah with a blessing on the fourteenth, and again, without a blessing, on the fifteenth, are Ashdod, Ashkelon, Beersheva, Beit She'an, Gush Chalav, Chevron, Haifa, Tiberias, Jaffa, Lod, Gaza, Acco, Tzefas, Ramlah and Shechem.

very same municipality, paying their taxes to it, and benefiting from its services.

❊ ❊ ❊

A shamefaced Jew approached Reb Shlomo Zalman on the last day of Pesach and confessed that he had forgotten to separate "*challah*" from the matzas that he and his family had been eating since the Seder.* At first the Rav was rather taken aback. "Just now, on the seventh day of the Festival, you remembered?!" The Gaon quickly overcame his astonishment and was able to share some very comforting news.

"I long ago adopted the policy of setting aside *challah* just before sunset on the eve of Pesach with the intention of including anyone who might have forgotten to observe the mitzva. It is reasonable to assume that by that very late hour everyone else would already have taken *challah*." His visitor was greatly relieved to hear this. It was unlikely that he would ever forget this mitzva again.

---

* It is a Torah commandment to remove a small portion from a batch of dough, to be consigned to the Priests. Nowadays, this is incinerated.

Reb Shlomo Zalman urged rabbis in various communities to adopt this same policy.

❊ ❊ ❊

Whenever Reb Shlomo Zalman needed to take a cab somewhere on a Saturday night, he would make certain to greet the driver with the customary "*Shavua tov,*" wishing the man a good week. He explained that if he said "*Shavua tov,*" the driver was certain to respond "*Shavua tov.*" In the event that the cabbie had not made *Havdalah*, by merely saying the words *Shavua tov* — according to one opinion — he may now be permitted to engage in labor (although he would still need to make *Havdalah*). Thus would the Gaon "turn the many to righteousness," minimizing transgressions wherever possible.

❊ ❊ ❊

Reb Shlomo Zalman's stringencies extended also to his personal attire. He had a special hat that he saved for bar mitzvas, weddings, and other joyous occasions. One day, on his way to a wedding, he had already descended the steep flight of steps from his house when he remembered that he had not changed his hat for the affair. Those who were accompanying him tried to convince the Rav that it did not matter, and when that failed, they offered to go back up for him and get his "simcha hat," but he wouldn't hear of it and insisted on getting it himself. Reb Shlomo Zalman maintained that to be appropriately attired was one of the ways in which he honored the bride and groom.

The Gaon was always cognizant of his attire, as befitted a Torah scholar. When he got dressed to go to the hospital, his last time to leave his house, he insisted upon wearing his Shabbos best, for Reb Shlomo Zalman knew that he would remain there over Shabbos. Family members brought him a sweater to wear but he refused to put it on because it had a stain.

One day a scholar escorting Reb Shlomo Zalman home noticed that the Gaon was straightening his clothes and arranging his hat squarely on his head as they approached his house. The escort was certain that the Rav was entertaining an important guest and asked him who it was.

Reb Shlomo Zalman replied with his warm, familiar smile that his wife was awaiting him. "The Talmud teaches that when husband and wife live properly together, the Divine Presence dwells in their abode. I am preparing myself for the *Shechinah*."

Surrogate Father

T THE AGE OF TWENTY, Reb Shlomo Zalman embarked on his first charitable enterprise, a *gemach* devoted to lending money to individuals who couldn't pay their annual rent (which according to Ottoman Law had to be paid in advance), or pay back their (usually non-Jewish) debtors. For eighteen years Reb Shlomo Zalman ran this interest-free loan fund, never once borrowing any of its funds for personal use,

although there were times when he more than qualified to do so. Moreover, an inspection of the fund's records revealed that operating expenses for things like paper or writing implements were never deducted.

When Reb Shlomo Zalman was asked about this seemingly egregious omission, he replied that he routinely covered those expenses from his own pocket since there would likely be times that he might inadvertently use a pen belonging to the *gemach* for his own personal use...

His philanthropic activities, of course, started long before the *gemach*. Legend has it that there was a police presence at his wedding, necessitated by the fact that some of the invited guests were convicts whom Reb Shlomo Zalman had befriended, and their prison furloughs had to be closely supervised.

Reb Shlomo Zalman was a rare *adam gadol* who personally ran a mega-empire of *chesed*. To anyone who gave him funds for charity — and there were many, as they had implicit trust in his honesty and ability to direct the money to the most deserving — he would stipulate, "I am accepting this with the understanding that I am to distribute it as I see fit."

To those who sought receipts, he said that they would be issued in the World to Come.

Quietly, without fanfare or public knowledge, Reb Shlomo Zalman married off orphans and other unfortunates, sometimes undertaking all the expenses involved. Occasionally a young man would visit the Gaon prior to his wedding and disclose his financial woes. The Rav, who listened patiently and sympathetically, would offer to cover the cost of furnishing the newlyweds' apartment. And needless to say, the furniture that was purchased was in stark contrast to that which comprised the "decor" of the Auerbach home.

Very, very few were privy to how Reb Shlomo Zalman managed his *chesed* empire. Hundreds of thousands of dollars went through his hands to the indigent and deserving. The Gaon had numerous innovative ways of getting the money into the pockets of those in need. He also had several emissaries to help him in the distribution effort, but he did not forgo his own role. A number of families would receive a regular visit from Reb Shlomo Zalman himself, who had not come to discuss the weekly Torah portion, and sometimes the Gaon would simply slip an envelope under the door.

No one will ever be able to quantify how much *chesed* Reb Shlomo Zalman did, for he worked "undercover," never seeking recognition. His foremost concern was that the recipient's privacy and dignity be maintained. Found among his records was a loan to a drug addict in the amount of NIS 1,500, lent on condition that he continue rehabilitation.

Reb Shlomo Zalman was perhaps most famous for his kindness to widows and orphans, but he sought out anyone in need. He would visit hospitals and old-age homes regularly, and it was not unusual to see him at a home for the mentally disturbed. Strain or inconvenience was never a factor when it came to visiting the sick or comforting mourners.

Reb Shlomo Zalman devoted his primary attention to embittered souls. The greater their affliction, the higher the priority which the Gaon awarded. A needy individual from a stable background would not receive as much attention as one with less wholesome credentials. Reb Shlomo Zalman liked the role of father, and felt very natural filling it for whoever was lacking a father of his own. Even if there was a father, but he was absent or far away, Reb Shlomo Zalman would take a fatherly interest.

To the American students learning in a yeshiva near his home, he exhibited exceptional concern. He always asked them specific questions about their progress in their studies, about their adjustment to yeshiva life in Israel, and about their families back home.

❋ ❋ ❋

Sometimes the families of those who excel in *chesed* pay the price. Many of us know individuals who are so devoted to helping others that if they are not out attending to the needs of the unfortunate, they are on the phone working out arrangements for the indigent. Between their acts of kindness, their own children are all but ignored, there is no one to help them with their homework or bathe them, and they eat their meals out of cans.

This was certainly not the case where Reb Shlomo Zalman was concerned. He was the active father of *every* family member, even distant relatives. When his brother-in-law was viciously knifed in the chest by an Arab terrorist, Reb Shlomo Zalman offered far more than get-well wishes. He was intimately involved in every aspect of Rabbi Prague's recovery; the Gaon spoke to medical authorities in Israel and around the world, questioning and consulting them about treatment and procedures to be followed, as there was no detail that he did not personally supervise. Just as a father would.

Reb Shlomo Zalman raised the Laizerzon family from the time that their father, another brother-in-law, passed away. He was a father to his nephews and nieces, seeing them all on a daily basis, yet he never even had to raise his voice. His look of displeasure was enough to elicit the desired behavior.

On Shabbos and Yom Tov, Reb Shlomo Zalman was particular to hand a slice of the challah he cut to his Rebbetzin and to his mother-in-law at *precisely the same time*, so that neither of the women he so highly respected would ever feel slighted.

So great was Reb Shlomo Zalman's concern for his relatives that he managed to honor his own parents not only during his exemplary lifetime, but after his passing as well: he instructed that his gravestone not be any taller than those of his parents who were interred nearby.

Ultimately, all Jews were Reb Shlomo Zalman's "family." When a group of Russian immigrant yeshiva students requested an audience with the Gaon, he welcomed the opportunity. Thirty newly religious young

Russians visited him in his home. They were received graciously and warmly and any request they made received his positive, enthusiastic reply. The Gaon wrote a letter on behalf of their yeshiva, spoke with the boys about their studies, encouraged them, allowed snapshots to be taken of himself with the students, and had he but been asked, would probably have danced the kazatska for them.

When Reb Shlomo Zalman was later asked about his zealous support of these boys, he replied simply that when he would be questioned in the World to Come about what he had done for Russian Jewry, he wanted to be sure he had done enough to give an answer.

Reb Shlomo Zalman was once walking along when he saw a disabled man stumble as he attempted to climb the stairs to his home. Without a moment's hesitation, the Rav hurried to his aid. There is no question that the Gaon's instincts were good; however, in this instance it might have been preferable to summon help. At the age of seventy-something his natural reflex to assist anyone in need was undiminished, but his physical capacity was not — the result of which was that the two men fell down the stairs together!

❊ ❊ ❊

An integral part of Reb Shlomo Zalman's *derech eretz* was identifying himself whenever he phoned. In this way he ensured that the person who answered the call would not suffer embarrassment over saying something he might not have said had he known who the caller was. The reasoning was certainly sound, although in practice it occasionally backfired, as in the time a child answered the phone and said her father was in the middle of learning and could not be disturbed. Reb Shlomo Zalman told her he would call again later.

After he hung up, the Gaon realized that the girl's father might be upset when he received his messages and feel he had dishonored the Rav. So Reb Shlomo Zalman called back earlier than he had said he would and made a point of telling the father how impressed he was by the child's respect for Torah study.

Whenever he was invited to be the *sandek* Reb Shlomo Zalman would always check with the baby's grandfather first to see if he minded forgoing the honor which was rightfully his.

Each time Reb Michel Gutfarb, Reb Shlomo Zalman's ailing *gabbai tzedakah*, was hospitalized for treatment, the Rav would call his home every other night to find out how *Mrs*. Gutfarb was doing. The strain she was under was taking its toll, but the voice on the line announcing, "This is Shlomo Zalman Auerbach" always lifted her spirits.

Reb Shlomo Zalman followed the progress of Reb Michel's illness, which would go into remission for a time after the treatments, only to recur. Reb Michel's physician in America said a transplant would be the only course of action should the disease reappear once again after treatment. Reb Michel dreaded this procedure and attempted to avoid it at all costs. To this end, fervent prayers were recited on his behalf around the world, but the doctor's grim prognosis would not be rescinded. A few years later, the symptoms returned.

Reb Michel's physician in New York, the foremost in his field, assured the Gutfarbs that the transplant was not only indicated but indeed was essential immediately.

As reluctant as Reb Michel was to undergo the procedure, his wife was even more reluctant for him *not* to undergo it. The consequences, she feared, would be calamitous. "You consulted the biggest doctor," she remonstrated with him, "and now you are obliged to consult the biggest Rav!"

Still loath to face the inevitable, Reb Michel phoned Reb Shlomo Zalman. The Gaon was as unequivocal in his ruling as the physician had been. "This is what the doctor says must be done, so it must, and right away!"

For the first time, Reb Michel disobeyed his Rav's *psak* — or would have, had the Gaon not hounded him daily, in the hospital and at home. He could not visit Reb Shlomo Zalman without being greeted with: "What are you doing here? I told you to go and have the procedure done!" He could not answer the phone in his home without hearing the Rav on the other end of the line, saying, "You're still there?! I thought you were already in the hospital!"

Reb Michel finally consented and, *baruch Hashem*, is here to tell the tale. Granted a new lease on life, he attributes his present good health to the unceasing paternal concern and loving encouragement of Reb Shlomo Zalman.

❊ ❊ ❊

When Reb Shlomo Zalman's daughter-in-law, Rebbetzin Rachel Auerbach, of blessed memory, lay in the hospital unconscious, her life in danger, her husband, Reb Shmuel

Auerbach, was hospitalized in Tel Aviv. Reb Shmuel's yeshiva, Ma'alos Ha-Torah, was left rudderless with no one at the helm. Reb Shlomo Zalman went there himself to see how the institution was getting along in their dean's absence. He approached one of the distraught students and said to him, "Do not let the *talmidim* here be foolish! Why should you be confused at a time like this? Now is when you must strengthen yourself in the study of our holy Torah and dedicate the time between study sessions to prayer." Afterwards, he asked permission to speak before the entire student body. As he stood on the *bimah*, everyone immediately gathered around him. He repeated what he had said to the first young man he'd spoken to, and then told this story:

"When Reb Naftali Trop, of blessed memory, fell ill, there was a great emotional awakening in Radin. Everyone volunteered hours of learning and prayer; everyone offered as much as he could to intercede on Reb Naftali's behalf in the Heavenly Court. When they went to the Chafetz Chayim, who deeply loved Reb Naftali, and asked him to contribute something towards Reb Naftali's welfare, he thought and thought. Finally, he announced that he would donate a moment of Torah for Reb Naftali. One moment of Torah study, he said! Do you know the worth of one moment of Torah? That is what he was willing to contribute. And from the Chafetz Chayim's one moment of Torah," Reb Shlomo Zalman continued, "the enthusiasm and commitment in the yeshiva became far greater than it had been up to that time."

Reb Shlomo Zalman's calm, quiet words gave *chizzuk* to Reb Shmuel's entire yeshiva.

Reb Shlomo Zalman had a firm policy that everyone — regardless of their religious or political views — was welcome in his home. People with whom he agreed, and those with whom he disagreed, all made their way to that humble house in Shaarei Chesed: from *talmidei chachamim* to secular politicians, from Rebbes to hoodlums, whoever wished to come was invited in.

In 1994, when a well-known Rebbe came to Israel to attend the inauguration of a new *beis midrash*, a delegation showed up at Reb Shlomo Zalman's door. The Rebbe and his *chasidim* had come to urge the Gaon to attend their *chanukas ha-bayis* and honor them by gracing the occasion with his presence.

Reb Shlomo Zalman demurred, saying he was old and weak. He wished them success in promoting a convocation that would bring about a glorification of God's name. But, regrettably, they would have to suffice with his good wishes.

This delegation, however, would not take "no" for an answer. To sweeten the pot they threw in a story that was certain to arouse the Gaon's sympathies. "There is a young man from this neighborhood about to be married," they told him, "who must raise so-much and so-much in order to be wed..." The *chasidim* had obviously done their homework: Reb Shlomo Zalman was indeed acquainted with the *chassan*-to-be. "Well, we would have no problem arranging to provide this money, that is, if the Gaon would honor us with his presence at the opening of our shul." It was an offer Reb Shlomo Zalman could not refuse.

Later, when asked why he had attended the function and spent so much time there, he replied: "I don't care at all what people say. I wanted to help this *bachur* and they provided me with the means to do so."

This was the guiding pattern of his life: his personal sacrifice was immaterial, as long as it enabled him to help others.

❈ ❈ ❈

In Reb Shlomo Zalman's early years as a Torah scholar, the Rothschild Foundation had earmarked a sizeable grant for a bright, young, candidate, and the search committee turned to Rabbi Yechezkal Abramsky for a recommendation. *Dayan* Abramsky's reply was immediately forthcoming: without a doubt, Reb Shlomo Zalman was his candidate of choice.

The candidate, however, turned down the nomination and refused to accept the money.

Confounded by these developments, the directors of the Foundation consulted with *Dayan* Abramsky. How would they manage to convince the reluctant award-winner to accept his award?

The dilemma required more intense consideration than the choice of a suitable candidate had. At last *Dayan* Abramsky came up with the answer. He told Reb Shlomo Zalman, "Other scholars, whose needs may be great, will surely suffer if you refuse this stipend. They will want to emulate your exemplary behavior in this matter as well, and as a result they and their families will be denied the financial assistance they so desperately require."

Nothing further needed to be said.

The Sensitivity of a Sage

 YOUNG JERUSALEM WOMAN became engaged, but not long afterwards she discovered, to her great chagrin, that her *chassan* was simply not what he had been made out to be, or what he had professed to be. All her life the girl had longed to wed a young scholar with a bright future in learning, a student who would diligently devote his days and nights to the study of Torah. But her *chassan*, she realized too late, had an entirely different agenda. She was devastated.

The father of the bride-to-be, seeing his daughter's distress, went to visit Reb Shlomo Zalman Auerbach to seek the Gaon's guidance.

The Rav listened to the sad tale and then, with somber gravity, recommended that the match be called off. "It is a מקח טעות — an invalid deal," he replied, using Talmudic legal terminology, "and should not be pursued lest the damage increase."

Before the father had even reached home to convey the *Gadol*'s advice to his daughter, the phone rang in his apartment and his son answered it. It was an elderly gentleman asking to speak to the *kallah*. "Who's calling, please?" her brother inquired.

"This is Shlomo Zalman Auerbach."

The boy quickly handed the receiver to his sister and she gripped it with trembling fingers.

The voice on the other end of the line was gentle. "Do not be distressed, my child, and do not worry," the Rav consoled her. "The day will soon come when you will begin a happy and joyous life with your true intended..."

❈ ❈ ❈

One of Reb Shlomo Zalman's favorite stories concerned an incident in the life of the Baruch Taam.* Shortly after the Baruch Taam concluded a *shidduch* for his son with the daughter of a wealthy man, a laborer in the community fell ill. The Baruch Taam had just learned of this tragedy when the future in-laws came to call. When the *mechutanim* saw how distraught the *chassan's* father appeared, they asked him with trepidation if he intended to cancel the *shidduch*.

"No, no!" the Baruch Taam assured them. "There is nothing further from my mind." He went on to explain that the cause of his distress was the illness of a local laborer, someone in his *kehillah*, and had nothing whatsoever to do with the *shidduch*.

Greatly relieved, his future *mechuteneste* remarked, "Of course we must pray for the poor man, but we need not be so upset, need we?"

When he heard this, the Baruch Taam did indeed cancel the *shidduch*! He maintained that if this woman had so little compassion, then he did not want his son to marry into her family.

---

* Rabbi Baruch Frankel, Rav of Leipnik, and famous father-in-law of Rav Chaim Zanzer.

This was the way Reb Shlomo Zalman educated the members of his family — not to greatness and leadership (although there is no doubt he did that by example), but rather to genuine compassion. As the Baruch Taam taught: One who does not feel the pain of others, is lacking not in *chesed* but in his very humanity — אין לו צורת אדם.

❀ ❀ ❀

An *avrech* in Reb Shlomo Zalman's neighborhood was in the midst of divorce proceedings when his father suddenly passed away. Because of his personal situation, of which his neighbors and friends were unaware, there was no one to provide him with a *seudas havra'ah* after the funeral. No one, that is, but Reb Shlomo Zalman. Realizing that the young man would be returning to an empty house and had no relatives to look after him, the Gaon himself prepared the traditional meal and waited for the mourner to come home so that he could serve it to him personally.

Due to unforeseen delays at the cemetery, however, Reb Shlomo Zalman ended up waiting for two hours outside, until he was able to fulfill this mitzva.

❀ ❀ ❀

The Sensitivity of a Sage / 255

Reb Shlomo Zalman was once invited to a wedding where the *chassan* was Sephardic. Naturally, the Rav received the honor of reciting a blessing under the *chuppah*.

He glanced around at the assembled guests, recognizing quite a few faces in the crowd. And then, to the astonishment of the predominantly Ashkenazic audience, he recited the blessing in the Sephardic pronunciation. It was his way of honoring the bridegroom and his family.

A member of the community who had suffered for many years in an untenable marriage, encountered a new set of complications when his wife refused to accept a writ of divorce. After expending a great deal of time and effort and enduring much heartache, he was finally able to acquire a *hetter me'ah rabbanim* — a dispensation signed by one hundred rabbis, releasing him from his marriage — which would allow him to begin living a normal life.

This rarely employed rabbinic dispensation, applied in extreme cases where the wife refuses to accept a divorce, required the validation of the Israeli Rabbinate, which meant that the man's travails had only just begun. The

Rabbinate was not quick to recognize the bona fide *hetter me'ah rabbanim*, although the document was signed by such notables as Reb Shlomo Zalman Auerbach. His "case" was placed at the bottom of the bureaucratic pile. The foreseeable likelihood of this fellow's marital status ever becoming officially certified as divorced was slim. In desperation he related his woes to Reb Shlomo Zalman.

A week after his meeting with the Gaon, a friend suggested to him that he try to arrange an appointment with the Chief Sephardic Rabbi, Rav Mordechai Eliyahu, who might be able to help expedite matters. Although the man was not Sephardic, he was desperate, and by this time willing to try any avenue that might lead him to freedom.

When he entered the Chief Rabbi's study and explained why he had come, Rav Eliyahu looked at him with surprise. "It was not necessary for you to trouble yourself to see me," he said. "Reb Shlomo Zalman has already called me on your behalf..."

A family of American visitors was staying in the Shaarei Chesed neighborhood for the summer. One day in shul, their nine-year-old boy, standing behind Reb Shlomo Zalman, was reciting the *Shemoneh Esreh* prayer quite intently. The youngster was still immersed in his devotions when Reb Shlomo Zalman finished his, and as a result the Rav was unable to take the final three steps back at the close of the prayer until the boy had finished.

When *Minchah* was over, the child's father approached Reb Shlomo Zalman to apologize for the inconvenience his son had caused. Seated nearby, he had witnessed the entire incident, but had been helpless to do anything about it.

Reb Shlomo Zalman was taken aback at the man's obvious discomfort. Not only did he feel that no apology was needed, but he assured the American that he had been overjoyed to see a young boy pray with such devotion. "Indeed," the Rav added, "I would like to thank you and your son for the inspiration."

❖ ❖ ❖

Once Reb Shlomo Zalman was riding in a taxi on his way to visit a child in the hospital, when he noticed an *avrech* along the way obviously headed in the same direction. He offered the young man a lift and the student gratefully accepted. En route, the Rav asked the taxi driver to stop so that he might buy a candy bar to give to the child.

After making his selection, Reb Shlomo Zalman hurriedly climbed back into the cab and began inspecting the label of the candy bar which he had just purchased. The *avrech* noticed the Rav's thorough inspection, and, being familiar with the product, he assured the Gaon that there was nothing to worry about. "The *hechsher* is a good one," he said, "and the Rabbi whose name is on it is reliable."

Reb Shlomo Zalman turned to him with a look of incredulity and said, "Oh, I wasn't examining the rabbinic supervision at all — I know it's kosher! I just wanted to make sure it's tasty."

❊ ❊ ❊

Reb Shlomo Zalman's daughter was preparing to travel abroad when her father telephoned and instructed her to postpone her trip for several days. "Of course I'll do as you request, Father," she said, "but why is a postponement necessary? Is everything all right?"

The Gaon patiently explained that since her daughter, who had just become engaged, was scheduled to spend her first Shabbos in her *chassan's* home, it was likely that she would want to share her impressions and feelings with her mother afterwards. "Why should you deny your daughter this opportunity?" he asked. "She needs you now — the trip can wait."

Over an extended period of time, Reb Shlomo Zalman carried on an important correspondence with the Chazon Ish, dealing particularly with the use of electricity on Shabbos. (Their correspondence appears in קובץ מאמרים בענין החשמל בשבת and in Reb Shlomo Zalman's *Minchas Shlomo*.) In the context of their deliberations, he visited the Chazon Ish on several occasions. Once the Chazon Ish was not at home when he arrived, but Reb Shlomo Zalman had the opportunity to converse with the Steipler, the Chazon Ish's brother-in-law, who was present. Their animated, companionable discussion proceeded until the Chazon Ish entered, whereupon both Reb Shlomo Zalman and the Steipler arose deferentially, and Reb Shlomo Zalman immediately followed the *Gadol* into his study. At the conclusion of their consultation, Reb Shlomo Zalman took his leave.

Some time later, Reb Shlomo Zalman suddenly recalled that when he had followed the Chazon Ish into his study, he had neglected to bid farewell to the Steipler. Fearing that he might have inadvertently offended the Steipler, Reb Shlomo Zalman immediately wrote him a letter of apology and sent it off by courier.

❈ ❈ ❈

It was well-known at the Kol Torah Yeshiva that during his *shiur*, Reb Shlomo Zalman would not entertain questions which related to a topic that he had already finished discussing. On one occasion, however, the students noted an unusual departure from this principle. A *talmid* had the temerity to raise just such a question, long after the Rav had proceeded to a different subject altogether.

In the brief silence that ensued, the students prepared themselves for the inevitable reaction, but to their surprise the Rav gave this *talmid* a lengthy, elaborate reply, and he did so with the utmost patience.

Later on, the *beis midrash* was abuzz with speculation as to the reason that the fellow had so easily been let off the hook. Had the Rav considered his query so incisive that it merited violating a sacrosanct principle? Hardly. Perhaps the Gaon felt he had not adequately explained the material and so he had taken this opportunity to do so? That suggestion was also dismissed; as always, Reb Shlomo Zalman had covered the subject thoroughly.

The reason soon became apparent: it was the very first time this student had raised a question since joining the *shiur*. That was sufficient justification for Reb Shlomo Zalman to be lenient and at the same time encourage the boy to participate actively in the lesson.

Every morning after services, Reb Shlomo Zalman would honor his sister with a visit. Widowed at an early age, she took great pleasure in preparing her brother's morning coffee (a gesture for which he had secured his Rebbetzin's gracious consent). He would further honor his sister by stopping at her home each Friday to taste the various dishes she prepared for Shabbos. And after the conclusion of Yom Kippur, one of Reb Shlomo Zalman's first calls would always be to his sister, to inquire how she had fasted.

Reb Shlomo Zalman's family was very important to him and his sister was but one of the relatives whom the Rav treated with affection and esteem. Whenever he attended a simcha, he made a point of wrapping up a piece of cake, putting it in his pocket, and taking it home for his elderly mother-in-law, in whose home the Auerbachs lived. In this small way, at least, she would be able to feel a part of the joyous affair which she could not personally attend.

❊ ❊ ❊

People's feelings and sensibilities were indeed the cornerstone of Reb Shlomo Zalman's halachic world. He was approached once regarding a communal dispute over whether the Shabbos service in a certain shul should start earlier or later on Friday nights.

Reb Shlomo Zalman ruled that they should definitely make the *daven*ing earlier, and that this is explicitly decided upon in the *Shulchan Aruch*. The delegates who brought this question to the Rav later consulted the *Shulchan Aruch* and could discover no such reference in either the laws of Shabbos or the laws of prayers.

Subsequent study revealed that it was a simple law germane to בין אדם לחברו — those laws which govern interpersonal relationships. One must always take the needs of family members into account. Earlier services would be less of a strain on the wives and small children waiting at home to begin the Sabbath meal.

❈ ❈ ❈

When I was getting married, I asked my friend, Prof. Shimon Glick of Beersheva, if he would mind driving Reb Shlomo Zalman to the wedding, knowing full well that the good professor would be getting the better part of the deal. He was only too happy to comply and said that although some of his children would be in the car, there would be plenty of room for the Rav to ride comfortably. He added that it would be his honor to provide this service for the Gaon and, at the same time, to do me this small favor.

In the midst of the affair, Prof. Glick's toddler daughter strayed over to the men's section and tried to join in the lively dancing. As the only female on that side of the *mechitzah*, her presence drew immediate attention.

The first men to spot the pint-sized intruder warned her that this territory was off-limits to her gender. Several overzealous fellows were approaching the child, preparing to summarily evict her, when Reb Shlomo Zalman caught sight of her. Gently he took the little girl and led her back to her mother.

※ ※ ※

There were two entrances to Reb Shlomo Zalman's house: the front entrance was up a steep flight of steps, and the back entrance was from the street. It would have made infinitely more sense for the Gaon to enter and exit at street level, but he refused to do so, despite the pain that walking and climbing steps caused him in his later years.

The reason he avoided the more convenient rear entrance was that it led through the room where his married son had been living ever since Rebbetzin Auerbach had passed away. Thus it was his son's room, and he would not infringe on the couple's privacy.

※ ※ ※

Perspiring and panting as he climbed the steep steps to the Gaon's house, Rav Eliezer Shach once commented, "To Reb Shlomo Zalman one must *ascend*."

Rav Yosef Shalom Elyashiv, שליט״א, with Reb Shlomo Zalman

Rebbetzin Leah Auerbach's father and father-in-law were the two greatest poskim *in Israel. Daughter-in-law of Rav Shlomo Zalman Auerbach, and daughter of Rav Yosef Shalom Elyashiv,* ליבחל״ח*, she did not have far to turn to solve any halachic problems — even in the event that her husband, Reb Ezriel Auerbach, an outstanding* talmid chacham *in his own right, were unable to resolve the matter.*

The story is told that she once entered an optometry store where the proprietor urged her to purchase a pair of glasses with photo-gray lenses. Aware of the halachic disagreement between her father and her father-in-law over the permissibility of wearing glasses on Shabbos which react to varying light intensities, Rebbetzin Auerbach had difficulty deciding whether to purchase them or not. The salesman was unable to understand her hesitation — Did she not want the finest optical lenses which were also inexpensive and convenient? The Rebbetzin explained her quandary: that her father was of one opinion on the subject, while her father-in-law held the opposite opinion.

The optometrist, frustrated over her vacillations, declared, "What difference do your father and father-in-law make? Go consult a posek*!"*

"Learn well and be happy."

Reb Shlomo Zalman praying at the cemetery on the Mount of Olives, overlooking the Kidron Valley and the Old City.

Greeting Rabbi Yaakov Perlow, שליט״א, the Novominsker Rebbe. At right, Rabbi Chaim Kreiswirth, שליט״א.

With Rabbi Chaim Pinchas Scheinberg, שליט״א, Rosh Yeshivah of Torah Ore.

With Rabbi Yaakov Kamenetsky, זצ״ל.

Reb Shlomo Zalman (accompanied by his son, Reb Baruch), greeting Reb Avigdor Nebanzahl, שליט״א, at the engagement of Rabbi Nebanzahl's son, Chizkiyahu.

The Gaon celebrates the Festival of Our Rejoicing

(R. to l.) Rabbi Moshe Shia Landau, זצ״ל, Rabbi Yonah Martzbach, זצ״ל, ליבחל״ח Rabbi Baruch Shimon Schneerson, (Rosh Yeshivah of Tchabin), and Reb Bezalel Zolti.

Reb Shlomo Zalman meeting with the Chief Rabbi of Jerusalem, Rav Yitzchak Kolitz, שליט״א, and the Rav of Shaarei Chesed, Rabbi Avraham Dovid Rosenthal, שליט״א. Arriving late to a Shabbos Ha-Gadol talk by Rav Kolitz, the Gaon was dismayed to see the audience rise in deference to him. From then on, Reb Shlomo Zalman would make certain to arrive 15 minutes early to Rav Kolitz's derashos.

At the bar mitzva of his grandson, Aryeh Leib Auerbach, teaching him how to properly lead the Birkas Ha-Mazon.

At the wedding of his grandson. Among those pictured: Rabbi Mordechai Auerbach, father of the groom; Reb Shlomo Zalman; ליבחלי״ח, *the Slonimer Rebbe, Rabbi Shalom Noach Barzevsky; the Bianner Rebbe; the Kashever Rebbe; Rabbi Avraham Yosef Laizerzon. Seated: the Vizhnitzer Rebbe of Netanya, Rabbi Adler, zt"l.*

Reaching out to all. Top: Testing the young students of Degel Yerushalayim on Tractate Shvi'is. Bottom: (r. to l.) Jerusalem Mayor Ehud Olmert; Jerusalem Deputy Mayor Rabbi Meir Porush; Assistant Director of Chinuch Atzma'i, Rabbi Avraham Yosef Laizerzon.

Reb Shlomo Zalman on his last Tisha B'Av.

With Reb Yisroel Gans (center) and Reb Aviezer Shapira, **Mashgiach** *of* **Kol Torah's** *Yeshivah Ketanah.*

Touchy Subjects

EB SHLOMO ZALMAN was always extremely careful to ensure the privacy of those who consulted him on personal matters. Never would a word escape his lips regarding the problems and issues that were brought before him. The domestic and marital difficulties of couples from very distinguished families came before Reb Shlomo Zalman, for his discretion was unimpeachable.

Once a woman came to see Reb Shlomo Zalman about a delicate matter. Rebbetzin

Auerbach informed her that the Rav was unavailable and would not have time to see anyone that day. She suggested it would be best to come back in a few days' time.

As the problem was pressing, the woman's husband went to seek the counsel of a different *rav*. Although the couple now possessed some rabbinical direction, the woman still wished to consult Reb Shlomo Zalman. At the precise time the Rebbetzin had recommended, she went to the Gaon's house and was admitted immediately.

The woman told Reb Shlomo Zalman that her husband had already spoken with another *rav* about the problem, adding that this *rav* had then related the entire matter to his wife. Unfortunately, the rabbi's wife, a woman not known for her reticence, had revealed this highly personal issue to others.

Reb Shlomo Zalman was aghast. "It is not permissible," he declared, "to consult a rabbi who divulges privileged information!"

This was Reb Shlomo Zalman's inviolate creed. When he sat down to lunch after a morning of seeing an endless stream of visitors, he would never even hint at what had passed between them or what problems they had unburdened on him. "*Tzurres,*" he would sigh sadly, "*tzurres!*" His empathy for the sufferers was great and often his brow would furrow with their worries, but his family knew never to press him. These private discussions which had transpired were between the petitioner, the Rav, and the Almighty.

Reb Shlomo Zalman would look down at the food his Rebbetzin had laid before him and ask rhetorically, "How can one think about eating when aware of the suffering that people endure?" Then he would answer his own question: "One must eat if one is to go on helping others and serving God."

So concerned was Reb Shlomo Zalman with ensuring his petitioners' privacy that he always destroyed the scores of letters he received daily after dealing with the problems they contained. After his passing, the only personal correspondence found in his study were the few letters he had not had a chance to attend to.

Sometimes Reb Shlomo Zalman would invite visitors into his private study to hear their halachic questions and problems. In the hallway leading to his room was a bookshelf, and one afternoon, as he ushered a guest down the corridor, the Rav came upon one of his grandsons, standing before the shelf and perusing the *sefarim*.

After seating his visitor, Reb Shlomo Zalman emerged from the room and asked his grandson to find a different place to stand. It was not that he suspected the young man of eavesdropping, God forbid, but rather Reb Shlomo Zalman was concerned that some of the people who came to speak with him might feel inhibited knowing that there was a third party within earshot.

A student who wished to see Reb Shlomo Zalman after *daven*ing in order to discuss a personal matter, approached the Gaon just as he was heading for home. Two men were arguing over which of them would have the honor of carrying Reb Shlomo Zalman's *tallis* home for him. Reb Shlomo Zalman was reluctant to choose between the two, and so when he caught sight of this student, he said, "Oh, here comes a disciple! He may carry my *tallis*."

As they made their way through the streets of Shaarei Chesed, Reb Shlomo Zalman and the student began to discuss the fellow's personal problem, but then the Gaon discerned that the other two erstwhile *tallis*-carriers were trailing behind. Concerned that they might overhear what was being said, he quickly grabbed the *tallis* from his student and thrust it into the hands of the man directly behind him. "Please be good enough to take the *tallis* up to my house right away," he said. "And would you," he added, turning to the second eager beaver, "kindly accompany him."

Thus Reb Shlomo Zalman was able to ensure privacy without hurting the feelings of the intruders.

Mrs. Cohen is a well-known *kallah* teacher who lives in Shaarei Chesed. In the course of her instructing young brides about the laws of family purity, questions would invariably arise. Mrs. Cohen took advantage of her geographic proximity to develop a perfect strategy for regulary receiving answers to her questions. Just as Reb Shlomo Zalman was descending the steps of his house on his way to yeshiva each morning, she would "ambush" him with one or two urgent questions. As he climbed into the waiting taxi, he would give her his replies.

One day Mrs. Cohen arrived even before the taxi, but after a few minutes' wait she realized that something was amiss. When she knocked at the door, Rebbetzin Auerbach explained that the Rav was feeling unwell and would not be going to Kol Torah that day.

Mrs. Cohen apologized for disturbing them, wished the Rav a speedy recovery and turned to leave. She did not get very far when she heard Reb Shlomo Zalman's voice beckoning her to remain.

"No, no," she protested, "I couldn't possibly bother the Rav when he is ill. Forgive me for intruding — I did not mean to impose."

The Gaon disagreed: his illness had not caused an imposition, he said, but an opportunity. "For once I am not in a rush and can answer your questions in a leisurely, more thorough fashion, as is their due."

I once was troubled regarding a match I had arranged between a yeshiva student and a convert. I knew that if I apprised the boy of the girl's background at the outset, chances were that he would be unwilling to date her.

However, I was convinced that once they had met and gotten to know one another, the boy would realize how wonderful she was and would not reject her over extraneous factors.

I had reasoned that it was important to "stack the deck" as much as possible in this girl's favor, but at the same time felt it was unfair to conceal information about her background from the boy until a commitment had already been made. I brought my dilemma to Reb Shlomo Zalman.

I could never have anticipated the Gaon's reaction. He did not see any drawback at all in revealing that the girl was a convert. "On the contrary!" he said with genuine wonder. "Can you imagine how fortunate he could be? Tell him he would have the privilege of fulfilling the mitzva of ואהבתם את הגר — the commandment to love the convert — every single day of his life!"

❉ ❉ ❉

Reb Shlomo Zalman was once sent a *she'elah* from abroad on a sensitive subject. The Rav responded that he was tending towards a stringent ruling on this matter: however, he added, "I prefer that you consult with the following halachic authorities [whom he knew to be lenient in this matter] and research the following sources," all of which he provided, "before pressing me for my opinion." At the end of the letter he added these words: "One who guards a mitzva will be spared from harm."

A similar story tells of someone who asked him a *she'elah* on an issue on which Reb Shlomo Zalman tended toward ruling stringently. Before rendering his decision, however, he urged this fellow to consult two other rabbis (whom he knew would be lenient).

When the petitioner returned to Reb Shlomo Zalman and related what these two rabbis had ruled, the Rav conceded that although he would have been stringent in this instance, he was clearly outvoted. "You must therefore accept the opinion of the majority," he declared.

❈ ❈ ❈

When the situation demanded it, Reb Shlomo Zalman did not hesitate to set aside his soft-spoken manner and use coercion. In 1978 an American boy was among the victims of a terrorist's bomb planted on a #12 bus to

Bayit Vegan.* The father of the boy, who was not (yet) religious, was a judge in the United States, a man who was well-known and well-connected.

Reb Shlomo Zalman had ruled that the boy was a *kadosh*, a sacred martyr of the Jewish People, and as such had to be buried in holy soil. The father would not hear of it. Irate, he phoned Reb Shlomo Zalman and, in a fit of rage, threatened to bring the full force of the United States legal authorities to bear, and to have his son's body removed under armed guard, if need be. One way or another, the dead boy would be flown "home."

"I do not doubt your ability to use your influence effectively," Reb Shlomo Zalman replied. "However, I must inform you that if you follow this route, I will let my opinion be known, and no Jewish burial society anywhere will inter your son."

Bearing in mind the bereaved father's emotional state, Reb Shlomo Zalman's tone became gentle as he offered his sincere condolences.

---

* Also among the victims was Reb Shlomo Zalman's nephew, Reb Aharon Meir, הי״ד, the son of Reb Refael Dovid Auerbach, זצ״ל.

He then patiently explained his ruling and emphasized why interment in the precious earth of the Holy Land was a glorification and an exaltation of the boy's soul.

The bereaved father relented.

Nothing Fancy

ATERIAL GOODS have little relevance to those who dwell in a lofty, spiritual dimension, yet their loved ones and devoted students feel driven to provide them with whatever small luxuries they deny themselves. It is an amazing, often ironic sort of give-and-take, wherein the recipient has no need or desire for the gift other than to honor the giver, and the giver — fully aware of this fact — still succumbs to his compulsion to give, as this is the only tangible

means he has of expressing his esteem for the recipient.

Thus did Reb Shlomo Zalman come to own a fancy, rather sophisticated telephone. His grandson had insisted on bringing back a gift for him from America, over the Rav's protests that the notion of the traveler, already burdened with the expense of his fare, feeling compelled to purchase presents for all and sundry was illogical. "A gift is going to be purchased for you regardless," the grandson pointed out. "Wouldn't it be less wasteful if it were something you actually wanted?"

Reb Shlomo Zalman could think of nothing that he lacked. "What do you suggest?" he asked with a shrug of his shoulders.

The grandson recommended a phone with an automatic redial mode (an option not available on Israeli-made telephones at the time), to spare the Rav the effort of repeatedly dialing the number of someone whose line was busy. The idea appealed to Reb Shlomo Zalman, who indeed begrudged the time wasted on such phone calls, but he would not give his consent until he was certain the device did not in any way disrupt the conversation of, or inconvenience, the party he was calling.

❊ ❊ ❊

I always asked the Rav if there was something I might bring back for him when I returned from one of my frequent trips abroad, perhaps something that was difficult to obtain in Eretz Yisrael. Each time I asked, the Rav's answer was the same: "There is nothing that I need," but I persisted nonetheless. Over time, the ritual became a polite means for informing the Rav that I would be absent from his *shiur* for the next few weeks.

On one occasion, to my amazement, Reb Shlomo Zalman's response to the by now routine question was positive, and he invited me up to his house. When I arrived, Reb Shlomo Zalman showed me a Shabbos candle holder of fairly common design — a cylindrical, spring-loaded metal tube intended to prevent the melted wax from dripping on the candlesticks — and explained that the spring mechanism was broken. He asked if it would not be too great an imposition for me to bring back two such holders from America.

Ecstatic over the opportunity to please my Rav and fill a genuine need, I would have scoured the earth to locate these candle holders, but this proved unnecessary. I had no difficulty in finding them at Eichler's bookstore in Flatbush. The new pair was an exact match to Reb Shlomo Zalman's broken one, and I joyfully carried my trophy home to Eretz Yisrael. Only upon unpacking my suitcase did I notice a tiny sticker on the base of the shrink-wrapped package that read: Made in Israel.

That the manufacturer was situated but a few blocks from Reb Shlomo Zalman's home in no way diminished my pleasure; in fact, it enabled me over the years to quite easily and surreptitiously replace all of the Rav's old, rusting candle holders with brand-new ones, plus a few spares.*

❊ ❊ ❊

Reb Shlomo Zalman lived in a modest, old house, another fact which, at the time of his passing, confounded the Israeli media accus-

---

* When I went to the Auerbach home to meet with Reb Baruch Auerbach as part of my research for this book, I noticed some of these candle holders lying on top of a cabinet in the Rav's study. Reb Baruch noted my interest and told me that I could have them if I wanted. "We have plenty," he said.

tomed to the more ostentatious lifestyles of politicians and public figures. Radio commentators were unable to conceal their bafflement as they described the throngs of mourners pouring into and around the rundown house this Torah giant had called home. Barred entry, they could not begin to imagine the simplicity and modesty of Reb Shlomo Zalman's residence, but those who were privileged to visit the Gaon in his lifetime can attest to its spartan decor. Every single item of furniture in the apartment was old and rickety — except for one: Reb Shlomo Zalman's chair.

Some years ago, the family decided that the Rav should have a "rebbishe" chair, so they bought him a sturdy wooden throne-like piece, with a firm back and armrests. No other chair in the house boasted armrests — and some did not even boast backs — but Reb Shlomo Zalman would have none of that. He had no need for such a "fancy" chair; it soon became a clothing valet in the bedroom. Later on, it proved useful for holding stacks of *sefarim*. Once a year the rebbishe chair would be unearthed — on Pesach, when it is halachically mandated to sit as kings at the Seder. That was the only time Reb Shlomo Zalman actually *sat* in the chair that had been intended for his daily comfort.

Another possession that made only a once-a-year appearance was a beautiful silver coffee pot which Reb Shlomo Zalman had inherited. This too graced the Rav's Seder table; for the rest of the year it was far too grand.

When the *chassan* of one of Reb Shlomo Zalman's granddaughters was invited to meet his illustrious future grandfather-in-law, Reb Shlomo Zalman was surprised to find the table laid with fine china. Unlike his own dishes, this set was perfectly intact and all the many pieces matched. It was apparent that the Rebbetzin, knowing that the young man came from a well-to-do family, had borrowed her neighbor's lovely china for this special occasion, and had prepared a lavish array of food to present thereon.

Reb Shlomo Zalman was swift to dispel any illusions of grandeur which this sumptuous spread might have created, and explained that usually, on a *Motza'ei Shabbos*, the Auerbachs were "just regular," nothing fancy. He went on to mention Rashi's comment on the verse where Avraham *Avinu* enjoins Sarah to serve their guests lavishly, saying: מהרי קמח שלש שאים — "Quick! [bring] three measures of flour..." Rashi explains that the reason Avraham had to expedite Sarah was because "A woman is not [by nature] generous with guests."

"The behavior of my Rebbetzin tonight," the Rav continued, "seems to contradict Rashi's observation, but I believe I can suggest a resolution: If a woman wishes to host her guests in a lavish fashion, she will do so but once a year, and the rest of the time she will be less generous. However, if she were to receive her guests in her regular, normal way, she would be pleased and able to do so all the time."

Awed as the young *chassan* must have been to find himself in the presence of the Gaon, he probably paid no attention whatsoever to the dinnerware. Just sitting at Reb Shlomo Zalman's table — not to mention, marrying his granddaughter — was fancy enough for anyone.

עיה"ק ירושלים תובב"א

ב"ה, יום

> Letter from Reb Shlomo Zalman to Rabbi Yerachmiel
> Fried, one of the Gaon's last letters, congratulating
> him on the birth of his daughter and praising
> the outreach program of the Dallas Kollel.

הרב שלמה זלמן אויערבאך
עיה"ק ירושלים תובב"א

ב"ה, יום

> Letter from Reb Shlomo Zalman to his charity fund
> treasurer and disciple, Reb Michel Gutfarb,
> wishing him well and offering
> his blessings for good health.

Letter from Reb Shlomo Zalman to Prof. Shimon Glick, director of the Ben Gurion University of the Negev Medical Center, permitting the use of morphine to relieve pain in terminal patients.

"Alimentary, My Dear Grandson"

FOR SEVERAL SUMMERS, Reb Shlomo Zalman would travel to Bnei Brak for his "vacation." This vacation consisted of spending a week at the Mishkan Shiloh Yeshiva, and never leaving the building. True, few Mediterranean breezes reached the *beis midrash* and no exotic flora flourished in the dim corridors, but for an active, prolific Rav whose attention was in constant demand, this yeshiva hideaway had a distinct advantage over most more popular vacation spots: it provided him with complete anonymity. His destination was a well-kept secret, so no one knew that the Rav was there (including those who attended the minyan in the building, who apparently did not recognize him), and thus he was able to study and think uninterrupted for the entire week.

His Rebbetzin did not join him for his summer retreats, but she carefully oversaw his departure. One year she caught him surreptitiously inserting two empty notebooks into his pocket. "I thought you were going on *vacation!*" she protested. "Now I see you are planning to spend it *writing!*"

Reb Shlomo Zalman offered an abashed look and made a hasty exit — taking two of his grandsons with him. They had a special part to play in this vacation.

Perhaps the primary reason that the renowned Reb Shlomo Zalman Auerbach was able to pass unnoticed at Mishkan Shiloh was the fact that the yeshiva catered to students of Yemenite descent, who were less likely to recognize the Ashkenazi Gaon. It was also the only reason that Reb Shlomo Zalman's vacation was ever less than perfect: the cook at Mishkan Shiloh, who was the wife of its

Rosh Yeshivah, was an expert at Yemenite cuisine; Reb Shlomo Zalman's palate, unfortunately, was not.

The *Rabbanit* cooked enormous quantities of food and always brought generous portions to Reb Shlomo Za'man's room for him and his grandsons. He was particular to finish everything that was served to him, lest he offend the *Rabbanit* or appear ungrateful. And this is where the two boys came in: their major responsibility for the duration of the vacation was food disposal. When their grandfather had consumed as much as he possibly could of the highly-spiced meal, the boys had to take over and deal with the rest.

One fateful day, the *Rabbanit* prepared a soup which was so heavily seasoned it could have heated the *beis midrash* of Kol Torah for the entire Jerusalem winter. Even before the first spoonful touched Reb Shlomo Zalman's lips, the aroma of its hot spices brought tears to his eyes. He replaced the spoon, took several deep breaths and tried again. It was hopeless. His lips refused to part at his command and his tongue clung in desperation to the roof of his mouth.

Reb Shlomo Zalman glanced at his grandsons briefly, and then shook his head.

He could hardly expect them to finish a soup which he could not even start. He turned to them once more, but their eyes, saucer-like with trepidation and their chins, trembling uncontrollably, aroused his avuncular compassion. With this avenue closed to him, the difficulty of food disposal became a seemingly insurmountable one, for Reb Shlomo Zalman's principles were inviolable.

The boys knew their grandfather was accustomed to working his way out of difficult problems, be they perplexing passages of Rambam or thorny issues of Halachah and technology; he was unlikely to be vanquished by a mundane matter of comestibles. The thought that *they* might have to provide the solution to his dilemma caused their stomachs to rise up in revolt.

But the Gaon was already trodding a different path in search of a resolution. He turned his analytical mind to the complexity at hand and began to dissect it. The reason he was unable to consume the consommé, he reasoned, was that it was generously laced with sharp condiments. If he could counteract the effects of those spices with, for example, something sweet, the resulting concoction might be more palatable. But where was he to find something sweet?

When Reb Shlomo Zalman's eye fell on the tall bottle of cola on the table, a small cry of triumph escaped his lips — and a loud gag of horror escaped the boys'! It was at times like these that they wished their grandfather would confine his innovative thinking to the realm of Halachah.

One can forgive the youngsters for their youthful ignorance, for clearly this *was* a matter of Halachah. What, indeed, was a little alimentary inconvenience compared to the enormous breach of *hakaras ha-tov* which the uneaten dinner might have caused?

Making a Point of Order

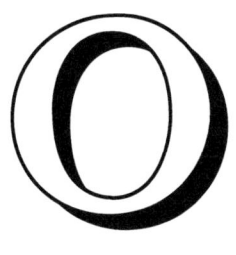NE OF Reb Shlomo Zalman's most noteworthy traits was orderliness. Everything in his life had its place and its proper priority. This is how he managed the uncommon combination of being a *Rosh Yeshivah* and educator of thousands of students, lecturer on the entire depth and breadth of the Talmud, and at the same time a *Posek* for all of world Jewry. It was in part through his tremendous sense of *seder* that he was able to excel in everything — Torah, *avodah*, and *gemilus chasadim* — and he strove to convey the importance of this trait to his students.

The Rav maintained that a yeshiva student must know how to do things at the right time and in the right place. When a young man comes to study in yeshiva, Reb Shlomo Zalman would say, he comes to learn, and not to perform acts of *chesed*. Opportunities to perform acts of kindness cannot be allowed to overshadow the student's primary goal of Torah study. Nevertheless, although learning must be his priority, without a doubt he must also find time for *chesed*.

❊ ❊ ❊

The Gaon disliked the currently popular practice in many yeshivas of "turning days into nights and nights into days." An oft-repeated story in the Auerbach household was about the Chafetz Chayim's personal routine: When acquaintances visited the Chafetz Chayim at home, as soon as the clock struck 10:30 P.M. he would say, "Tomorrow is another day," and leave the room.

The Auerbachs adopted this practice as well, and at ten-thirty, the family members would say to one another in Yiddish, "*Morgen iz oich a tog*," and at that moment all activity would come to a halt. Reb Shlomo Zalman would repair to his room and not reappear until the morning. What he did inside his room, and at what hour he actually went to sleep, no one ever knew, but as far as the family was concerned, the day ended at ten-thirty.

❋ ❋ ❋

Reb Shlomo Zalman would often quote the opening phrase of the *mishnah*, תנא, כיצד סדר הסיבה — "We have learned: What is the order of leaning..." as proof that it was fundamental Halachah and Tannaitic propriety to focus upon order.

Once when the Rebbetzin fell ill, Reb Shlomo Zalman assumed all of his wife's responsibilities. He did not want the children to realize that their mother was so sick. Homemaker, cook, babysitter — he did it all, *without* altering his own schedule of delivering six lectures a week for two hours each... for a period of *five months*!

Decades later, when the Rebbetzin passed away, Reb Shlomo Zalman began doing the household grocery shopping at the local store. To ease the burden on the Rav, the shopkeeper offered to deliver the groceries, but Reb Shlomo Zalman, always reluctant to impose on others, said, "I see that you wish to perform a *chesed* for me, and I am most grateful, but I would much prefer that you learn *mishnayos* to glorify my wife's soul."

Reb Baruch, the Gaon's youngest child, moved into his father's house with his family after the passing of the Rebbetzin. Even with Reb Baruch and his devoted family's constant presence and assistance, Reb Shlomo Zalman still looked after the daily operation and expenses of the household so that he would not have to burden others.

As a permanent resident, Reb Baruch was privileged to have not only the greatest share of *kibbud av* but also the greatest exposure to the Gaon's talent for investing every action — even the most mundane — with ingenuity. He applied this talent, for example, even to the way he distributed candies to his grandchildren.

Rabbi Michael Schoen once noticed a local handyman at work in Reb Shlomo Zalman's house, repairing the Gaon's Chanukah menorah, just in time for the Festival. Having tried in vain to get this very fellow to repair some items in his own house, Rabbi Schoen joked, "Now I see what it takes to get you to fix something!"

The handyman replied matter-of-factly, "If you had reminded me repeatedly since the month of Elul, three months ago, I would have fixed your things by now too..." Apparently, for those who live an orderly existence, it is possible to prepare for a holiday well in advance.

❈ ❈ ❈

Reb Shlomo Zalman's sense of order and sensitivity to others dovetailed when it came to attending weddings. He was always very gracious about accepting invitations to attend the simchas of acquaintances, but for some time had been vexed by the dilemma of how long to remain at the affair. How much time could he spare from his pressing obligations? How brief could his attendance be without offending his host?

The Rav reasoned that to put in a cameo appearance for but ten minutes was insulting, yet to remain for a full half hour was too great a demand on his time. He finally resolved the dilemma by allocating a time slot of between fifteen and twenty minutes.

[Author's note: A student of Reb Shlomo Zalman's was present in the home of Reb Moshe

Feinstein when the famous *Gadol* sighed, "I have a hard day ahead of me. I have two queries to which I must respond: one is easy and one is difficult. The easy one is regarding a *kohen* who is married to a divorcee; the difficult one is from Reb Shlomo Zalman Auerbach, who has written to inquire until what age one must participate in simchas."]

❋ ❋ ❋

In Bnei Brak, former students of Kol Torah established a *beis midrash* for themselves, and consulted Reb Shlomo Zalman concerning every aspect of the project. At one point, they thought to establish a "Shabbos *kollel,*" and set a regular time for learning together. When they presented the idea to the Rav, he immediately asked when the *sedarim* would be. "We were thinking of learning for an hour immediately after Shabbos morning services," the young man began.

"No, that's impossible," the Gaon interrupted. "You cannot keep your wives waiting after *Shacharis.* They want to hear Kiddush and eat. You should learn for an hour *before* services."

At his interlocutors' look of dismay, Reb Shlomo Zalman asked, "What is the problem?

In the summer there is time to rest in the long afternoons, and in the winter the nights are long enough for you to get plenty of sleep on Friday night. In addition," he continued, "you can learn for half an hour before *Minchah* on Friday afternoon."

"But what can we accomplish in half an hour?" the young men asked.

"You can learn *Musar*, of course. Half an hour is perfect for *Musar*."

The Kol Torah graduates were surprised. They had never heard of *sedarim* like these, but if the Gaon had decided, there was nothing more to say.

And so it remains to this day. At the *beis midrash* of Kol Torah graduates in Bnei Brak, all the *avrechim* come to learn an hour before *Shacharis* on Shabbos mornings and half an hour before *Minchah* on Friday afternoons.

Amazing Grace

EVERYONE ASSUMES THAT Adam's singular transgression was that he ate from the tree that was forbidden to him. Reb Shlomo Zalman maintained that there was a *different* offense for which he was guilty, one which precipitated his violation of the ban on eating from the tree. His crime was not expressing his gratitude to God for presenting him with a wife. (See Rashi on *Bereshis* 3:12.)

Reb Shlomo Zalman was always very appreciative for any favor that was done for him and he never forgot to articulate his gratitude. One of the greatest favors one could do for the Rav was to drive him home from the Yeshiva. While there was considerable competition for this honor, Reb Shlomo Zalman viewed it as a *double* favor: for him, since he realized his house was out of the way for the driver; and for the Yeshiva, which was spared the taxi fare.

Reb Shlomo Zalman would always devote his undivided attention to his driver, in appreciation of the kindness extended to him. Rabbi Yerachmiel Fried was one of the lucky ones privileged to drive the Gaon once a week. Rabbi Fried managed to utilize this precious time effectively enough to produce a *sefer, Yom Tov Sheini K'hilchaso*, based on the questions he posed and the answers he received during the rides.

❉ ❉ ❉

Rabbi Eli Baruch Finkel was very surprised to see Reb Shlomo Zalman arrive at his son's bar mitzva. Needless to say, he was also extremely delighted, but he had no idea why the Gaon would go to so much effort, traveling all the way from his neighborbood to a distant part of town on a late *Motza'ei Shabbos*.

When asked why he had troubled himself so to attend the simcha, Reb Shlomo Zalman replied succinctly, "*Hakaras ha-tov.*" No one, including Rabbi Finkel, had any idea what the host had done for the Gaon that merited such an expression of appreciation. But that, of course, was due to the fact that most people have a frame of reference different from that of Reb Shlomo Zalman, at least when it came to gratitude. True, Rabbi Finkel had never done anything for Reb Shlomo Zalman personally, but he had been the *shadchan* for one of the Rav's *grandsons*. The Gaon was happy for the opportunity to express his appreciation to the successful matchmaker.

There would yet be another opportunity when Rabbi Finkel would be able to benefit from that good will. He was about to depart to America to officiate at a wedding, when a startling thought occurred to him. The fact was, he had never officiated at a wedding before, and the Talmud teaches, "Whoever is not thoroughly familiar with the laws and precepts of marriage and divorce should not involve himself with them."

Rabbi Finkel opened up the *Shulchan Aruch* and, for days before his departure, studied the Laws pertaining to marriage. He jotted down twenty practical questions that can and often do arise at wedding ceremonies. And the following morning he went to Reb Shlomo Zalman to pose his twenty lengthy and complex questions.

With wisdom and patience, Reb Shlomo Zalman explained the Halachah and told him which practices to observe regarding each question. The Rav's response took no less than *two hours!* When the lesson ended, Rabbi Finkel confessed with full candor that if he didn't write down immediately everything that he had heard, he was liable to forget something important. The Gaon rose from his seat in his study and insisted that Rabbi Finkel take it and work at the desk. "I'll find myself a place [to receive the others who had lined up in the interim]," the Gaon said. The number of people waiting outside kept growing, but Rabbi Finkel remained where he was, transcribing what had been told to him for the next hour and a half, in addition to two lengthy interruptions for further clarifications.

❈ ❈ ❈

Mrs. Leah Oppenheimer relates that in all the times that the Gaon rode with her and her husband in their car, Reb Shlomo Zalman never once forgot to acknowledge her presence with his gracious smile and a "How are you?"

When they reached their destination, invariably a crowd would swarm around the vehicle and people would rush over to open the door and escort Reb Shlomo Zalman to the function. If in the tumult of the crowd and the vying for his attention the Rav would forget to take his leave of her (he *never* forgot to thank his driver), he would return to the car, beg Mrs. Oppenheimer's forgiveness and bid her good-bye.

Reb Shlomo Zalman had close ties to Shaare Zedek Medical Center in Jerusalem, a relationship that went back many years. Any complicated questions germane to Halachah were brought before the Gaon, and the hospital's Rabbi-in-residence is Reb Shlomo Zalman-approved. When the Yom Kippur War broke out, Reb Shlomo Zalman reported for duty at the hospital. "I know that a lot of questions will arise," he said. "Better that I be here than that you should have to go looking for me."

After the passing of Dr. Falk Schlessinger, the presidium of Shaare Zedek sought to appoint a not-(yet)-religious doctor from abroad to be the new hospital director. Reb Shlomo Zalman was adamantly opposed to this move and tried in every way possible to prevent its actualization. He feared that under the leadership of a non-religious administrator, the very nature of the medical center would alter irrevocably. (When this possibility arose again years later, Reb Shlomo Zalman invited Professor Shimon Glick from Beersheba to Jerusalem, to try and interest him in accepting this position — to no avail.) The Gaon's efforts to block the appointment of this secular physician seemed to be in vain. When all else failed, he even wrote a letter to the candidate, who was still abroad at the time, requesting that he remain where he was.

Soon after, this same individual showed up at Reb Shlomo Zalman's door and the Gaon invited him into his study. At the conclusion of their meeting, Reb Shlomo Zalman graciously escorted the doctor out, affording him the fullest honor. He even walked the guest all the way down the steep staircase from his home to the street.

The family members present were incredulous. Their father's opposition to the man's appointment was certainly no secret, yet his behavior had been anything but antipathetic.

Reb Shlomo Zalman could not understand what they could not understand. "True, I consider him unsuitable to direct a religious institution," the Gaon said, "but personally I have nothing against him..."

For a long time Reb Shlomo Zalman suffered from an extremely painful muscle disorder in his face. The pain he experienced was so excruciating that it was not unusual to see him crying out and clutching at his face in the middle of learning. If he experienced a muscle spasm during the course of a lesson, he would leap up as though bitten by a snake, and as soon as the pain subsided he would continue right where he had left off, with his usual smile, as if nothing had happened. On numerous occasions he explained that his misery was greater than having ten daggers thrust into his cheek.

Because the pain was so unbearable he agreed in 1964 to undergo delicate neurosurgery. There was significant risk involved, including the danger of side effects. (As a result of the operation, his hearing in one ear and his sight in one eye were impaired, and half his face was paralyzed.)

The morning of the operation, his family gathered around their beloved father with anxiety and concern permeating every fiber of their being. Reb Shlomo Zalman waited patiently for the scheduled hour of his surgery, engaged in a heated discussion with his brother-in-law, Rabbi Avraham Horwitz, over an intricate matter of Halachah. When the Rav's turn was called, Rabbi Horwitz walked alongside him toward the operating theater, the entire time engrossed in this thorny halachic matter.

At the very threshold of the operating room Rabbi Horwitz, with a very heavy heart and eyes swimming with tears, took leave of his brother-in-law. Reb Shlomo Zalman failed to notice this, as he stood facing the *mezuzah*, contemplating. Suddenly he turned to Rabbi Horwitz, who immediately drew near, his arms outstretched to embrace the Gaon and his moist eyes full of compassion and love.

In a calm, steady voice, Reb Shlomo Zalman added a different insight to the matter they had been discussing. As everyone around stood trembling with trepidation and apprehension, the Rav remained an island of tranquillity. His mind and emotions had been purified of fear by the study of Torah.

The surgery was performed on a Sunday and Reb Shlomo Zalman let it be known that he intended to spend that Shabbos at home. Reb Shmuel tried desperately to dissuade his father: It was rather evident that after undergoing such a difficult operation, the wise thing to do was to remain under hospital supervision. Logic, for once, did not prevail; Reb Shlomo Zalman refused to give in.

Reb Shmuel felt he had no recourse but to apply the kind of pressure his father would be unable to resist. He went to see the Tchabiner Rav, Dov Berish Weinfeld,* a very close friend of the Gaon's, and apprised him of his father's intentions. The Tchabiner Rav instructed Reb Shmuel: "Tell your father that I love him as much as I love myself, and I insist that he stay in the hospital over Shabbos!"

How could the Gaon refuse his dear friend?!

---

* In his eulogy for his father, Reb Shmuel quoted the Tchabiner Rav who, forty-five years earlier had said: "There is not the minutest element of any *psak* that Reb Shlomo Zalman has ever issued that I have any doubts about."

A Unique Life-Support System

EB SHLOMO ZALMAN'S concern for his fellow Jew knew no bounds. Old, young, Sephardic, Ashkenazic, religious, not (yet) religious, Israeli or member of the Diaspora, he cherished them all. When it came to the plight of a widow or an orphan he had no peer and his efforts on their behalf extended well beyond the ordinary limits of *chesed*.

One day Reb Shlomo Zalman was told about the death of a *ben Torah* whose wife had given birth that very same day. Reb Shlomo Zalman was horrified by the tragedy. He asked Reb Michel Gutfarb, his trusted charity assistant, to drive him to the bereaved mother, for he had to visit her right away.

This was Reb Shlomo Zalman's standard policy. He never delayed performing a kindness or put off a *chesed*. One of the guiding principles in his life was the Rabbinic dictum: מצוה הבאה לידך אל תחמיצנה — "Do not forgo a mitzvah that falls into your hands."

Reb Shlomo Zalman arrived at the hospital maternity ward and sat with the woman for a full hour, trying (and succeeding) to raise her spirits. At the end of the visit he announced that from that moment on he intended to be the "father" in the family and he wished to be apprised of any and every problem that might arise. Then, with a smile on his face, he announced that it was the father's privilege to see his son, and he asked the mother to show him the newborn baby.

❦ ❦ ❦

A young Jerusalem yeshiva student suddenly passed away, leaving behind a wife in an advanced stage of pregnancy. The *avrech's* young widow was beside herself with grief. Reb Shlomo Zalman was determined that even without a husband she would never feel that she was alone. The renowned sage told her that he wished to be informed when she went to the hospital to give birth.

The time arrived and the doleful woman was in a turmoil of emotion. Her tears were a bittersweet mixture of joy and sorrow. The joy that a mother should feel at childbirth was overshadowed by the realization that her baby would never know its father. How agonizing it was to go to give birth all by herself, with no husband to accompany her, and to know that there would be no excited new father to greet his wife and baby afterward.

Her body racked with contractions, her mind driven by sorrow, all the hospital staff shared her anguish. And then the champion of widows and orphans arrived! Reb Shlomo Zalman wanted to be the first to wish her *mazal tov*, and he used the opportunity to provide a little grief-counseling as well. In no time Reb Shlomo Zalman had seen to it that the birth was truly a joyous occasion.

❈ ❈ ❈

Reb Shlomo Zalman once noticed an eight-year-old boy reciting Kaddish in shul. The boy's pronunciation was atrocious and the tune that he used to recite the prayer was also incorrect. The little boy obviously understood that his Kaddish was flawed, for he appeared very uncomfortable reciting it, and his attendance in shul was sporadic.

Reb Shlomo Zalman approached the boy, sat down with him, and patiently and gently explained to him the meaning of the Kaddish prayer for the deceased. The next time the two met, the Rav explained on a third-grade level what is achieved for the soul of the departed by reciting Kaddish regularly. Reb Shlomo Zalman utilized the next opportunity to teach the boy how to pronounce the Aramaic words correctly, and how the prayer is traditionally chanted. By the time he had finished his final lesson, the boy was a regular attendant, for he could not dream of denying his father's soul the benefits that only he could provide.

When an *avrech* died, leaving a widow with many children, two of whom were retarded, Reb Shlomo Zalman mobilized immediate relief. He called up his trusted aide, Reb Michel

A Unique Life-Support System / 317

Gutfarb, and instructed him to raise a very significant sum to help out this family. And Reb Shlomo Zalman had set his sights very high.

Reb Michel accepted his Rav's difficult charge, knowing full well that he had a tough challenge ahead of him. The next day Reb Shlomo Zalman phoned Reb Michel and told him that he also wanted to do his share of this mitzva, and was personally pledging $15,000.

No one knew better than Reb Michel how much Reb Shlomo Zalman had devoted himself to helping out the poor and the unfortunate, causing the hearts of both widows and orphans to rejoice. But in this instance, which tragically was not all that much more calamitous than the other projects in which Reb Shlomo Zalman routinely became involved, there appeared to be an added incentive. Reb Michel asked the Gaon to elaborate.

Reb Shlomo Zalman explained that the widow was not an emotionally stable woman. He had once seen her enter the synagogue and embarrass her husband terribly in front of a crowd of people. How had the husband, of blessed memory, responded? He hadn't said a word. "I witnessed this nobility with my own eyes," Reb Shlomo Zalman told Reb Michel, "and now I feel duty-bound to honor the man's memory with generous assitance."

Rabbi Moshe Shia Landau was "the" disciple of the Chazon Ish. He had spent days and nights in his master's presence, absorbing the warmth and direction of the *Gadol Ha-dor*. But those days of splendor, basking in the glow of the Chazon Ish, discussing intricate Torah concepts and observing his every move, now seemed a million years away to the Torah giant who was admitted to the hospital suffering from a terminal condition. What remained of Reb Moshe Shia Landau was a wasted man connected to multiple life-support systems.

When Reb Shlomo Zalman came to visit him in the hospital Rabbi Landau was very weak and fighting tenaciously to stay alive. The day of the visit was but one day before Rabbi Landau's demise.

As soon as Reb Shlomo Zalman entered the ward, Rabbi Landau took the opportunity to ask the Gaon's forgiveness for arguing against him in his *sefer* on *Shvi'is*. Reb Shlomo Zalman could see no grounds for Rabbi Landau to request forgiveness. It was a *machlokes l'shem Shamayim* — "a dispute for the sake of Heaven," he said. "If you feel that you must ask forgiveness from me, then by the same reasoning, the Ravad would have to ask forgiveness from the Rambam for arguing against what he wrote! But of course, such is not the case.

"So, there is no need for you to ask forgiveness. However, you are absolutely wrong in your opinion and in the reason that you differ!" Reb Shlomo Zalman grew heated in his rejection of Rabbi Landau's arguments. The latter barely had the strength to respond, yet an intense debate ensued. Reb Michel, who had accompanied Reb Shlomo Zalman, felt compassion for poor Rabbi Landau.

At the end of the visit, Reb Shlomo Zalman rushed out of the ward and searched for the doctor who was treating Rabbi Moshe Shia Landau. When he finally caught up with the professor, he recommended what measures he thought should be implemented and where he thought the treatment was lax. The doctor took heed of the distinguished rabbi's words, but noted that he did not in all honesty believe that Rabbi Landau would survive that night.

Reb Michel was witness to things he had never seen before: How an *adam gadol*, forever concerned with the needs and sensitivities of others, performs the mitzva of visiting the sick. Reb Shlomo Zalman perceived that under the tubes and intravenous lines was a Jew who craved to fight the *milchamta shel Torah*, engaging in the rigorous debate of halachic issues that had been the very essence of his life. All of the resuscitation devices in the hospital could not provide the give-and-take of learning — the very oxygen of life — of which he was currently denied.

Up until then, whoever visited Rabbi Landau assumed that he was too frail to carry on a discussion about learning. And this deprivation of what was most critical to him, pained him the most. Reb Shlomo Zalman wished to prove to Rabbi Landau that he still had reason to live. If Reb Shlomo Zalman Auerbach could still argue with him as vigorously as though they were in a *beis midrash*, it would bolster the patient's self-worth and provide a tremendous boost of encouragement. To argue with a man whose vital signs were but a faint flutter was not in Reb Shlomo Zalman's nature, but nothing was more natural for the man than to take care of others' needs.

And that is why his "visiting the sick" did not begin with platitudes and end when he

A Unique Life-Support System / 321

exited the ward. His was not just lifting the spirits and providing good cheer; he had to attend to all the needs of the sick. He had to personally verify that the medical care being provided was optimal — even in the case of a man just hours before his passing.

Of course, verifying and ensuring that top medical care was being provided was an august undertaking which could not have been carried out without the participation of several assistants. Rebbetzin Miriam Lubling and Rabbi Yosef Mayer of Brooklyn, New York, were two main aides in this enterprise.

At the Gaon's word, Rebbetzin Lubling would immediately marshal her myriad connections in the medical world. Likewise would Rabbi Mayer, *menahel* of the Sha'arei Yosher Yeshiva in Boro Park, raise huge sums of money if Reb Shlomo Zalman felt there was a need.

❃ ❃ ❃

Reb Shlomo Zalman once dispatched Reb Zvi Weisfish, *Rosh Yeshivah* of Yeshivas Ha-Ran, to visit an elderly *talmid chacham* who was hospitalized in Hadassah Hospital. Reb Shlomo Zalman instructed Rabbi Weisfish exactly how to lift the man's spirits. He revealed that this aged *talmid chacham* was bitter over the fact that he had never been offered a teaching position. "I would like you to offer him a position in your yeshiva, to commence as soon as he recovers. It may just help..."

It was well known in Reb Shlomo Zalman's neighborhood of Shaarei Chesed that if you wished to be graced by a visit from the great Rav all you had to do was to feel unwell.

Reb Shlomo Zalman once went to visit a sick person who lived on one of the upper floors of an apartment building. The Rav himself was elderly, and the ailing man's family knew that it would be difficult for him to climb all the stairs, so they placed a chair on each landing for him to sit on and rest on the way up. Now, sitting down and standing up was more difficult for the Rav than simply stopping on each floor to catch his breath, but since the people had put the chairs there out of consideration for him, he used them.

❊ ❊ ❊

When Reb Shlomo Zalman heard the heartrending story of a recently widowed mother of nine children in America, the Gaon was so distraught over the plight of this poor woman that he acquired her phone number and called her long-distance. He introduced himself as Shlomo Zalman Auerbach, but the name did not elicit any sign of recognition. He tried again, this time adding, "This is Shlomo Zalman Auerbach — from Jerusalem..."

"Oh!" came the astonished response from the other side of the Atlantic.

He consoled this woman, a total stranger, for twenty minutes, and then he said a few words to each of her children. To the youngest he said: "When you return to *cheder* tell all your friends that Reb Shlomo Zalman called you up and spoke to you from Yerushalayim."

The Gaon knew just how to speak to everyone: to rebbes, yeshiva students, strangers, and even little children. Everyone.

❊ ❊ ❊

Reb Shlomo Zalman's method of comforting the bereaved was unique and not readily understood by many. A prevalent practice is that only the very closest relatives and friends come to comfort mourners during the first three days of the *shivah* period. Furthermore, one visiting a house of mourning should not speak until the mourner initiates conversation.

Invariably, Reb Shlomo Zalman would come to comfort the mourner during the first, or at the latest, the second day of *shivah*. He also would be the one to open the conversation. The rationale behind his actions was that he was well aware of how much his presence could contribute to lifting the spirits of the bereaved and bringing solace to the mourner. Since he was conscious that he had something significant to contribute, he wished to offer it when it would be needed the most. And unlike many who pay condolence calls at hours that are convenient for *them*, Reb Shlomo Zalman was careful to visit the bereaved only at times that would not disrupt their personal schedules or inconvenience them in any way.

Reb Shlomo Zalman always wanted people who came to him with their sorrows or sought his advice to follow up their visit with a report of the outcome. If they failed to apprise him, he would find a way to discover the outcome on his own, unless the matter was of a very personal nature, in which case he realized that his interest could cause them embarrassment.

On one occasion someone told Reb Shlomo Zalman of the appalling plight of a particular woman. Several weeks later the situation straightened out and disaster was averted. When Reb Shlomo Zalman called up the family member who had brought him the bad tidings, to inquire how matters were developing, he was elated to hear the good news. After offering a heartfelt blessing that the family be spared any future hardship, he added that it would have been far more appropriate for him to have been informed of the good news without having to do his own research. "You could have spared me untold grief, for I have been agonizing all this time over her plight."

At a bris, a guest stopped Reb Shlomo Zalman and related a tale of woe. "The hospital refuses to perform surgery on me until they first do a lengthy, unnecessary procedure, and meanwhile my situation is worsening from day to day."

Reb Shlomo Zalman accelerated the meal at the bris and quickly took his leave in order to intervene at the hospital. The head of surgery was very surprised to receive a visit from the distinguished rabbi. He explained to the Rav that his patient's current condition would make performing the operation dangerous. It also turned out that the matter wasn't urgent at all. Reb Shlomo Zalman had heard all he needed to know. He returned home untroubled and content with the knowledge that this Jew was not being denied vital medical attention.

Outpatient

IT WAS FRIDAY AFTERNOON, eve of one of the shortest *Shabbosim* of the year, in Jerusalem's Shaare Zedek Medical Center. Outside, there was a flurry of activity as people scurried to hail taxis and pile onto the last bus of the day. Inside, the hospital lights seemed a bit less fluorescent, the climate remotely controlled, and the slow-paced tranquillity of the Sabbath schedule was already descending upon the near-empty corridors of this very modern urban medical facility.

Out of the corner of his eye Reb Michel Gutfarb thought he saw a very famous personage padding down the corridor.

"It can't be," he told himself, quickening his gait. But just to make sure, he looked again. And yes, there he was. Scarcely an hour before candle lighting, Reb Shlomo Zalman was making his way toward the bank of elevators.

Their eyes met and Reb Shlomo Zalman rerouted himself to catch up with Reb Michel. Needless to say, Reb Michel practically galloped over to the venerable sage to spare him the exertion, and deferentially inquired what had brought him to the hospital.

Reb Shlomo Zalman explained that he had come to visit someone two hours earlier, but when he'd seen how lonely the patient was, he felt he could not abandon him after a normal-length visit.

"Since I am already here," Reb Shlomo Zalman added, "maybe you know of some other patient I am acquainted with whom I could visit?"

Reb Michel glanced quickly at his watch. It was sixty-five minutes before candle lighting, little time for the Gaon to get home and prepare for Shabbos. On the other hand, he knew of someone in the hospital who was indeed aching for such a visit.

After brief deliberation, Reb Michel gently guided Reb Shlomo Zalman along while telling the sage about an encounter he had just had.

"I was walking through one of the wards when I spied a new patient with a *kippah* on his head. I asked him if he'd had a chance to put on *tefillin* today, implying that I would be happy to help him if he so desired.

"The fellow scowled. An expression of disgruntlement registered on his face, indicating that he had entered the cantankerous period of his hospital stay. The man was obviously suffering and I realized that whatever I said or offered would have elicited a similar reaction.

"'Whom do you think you're talking to?' he grumbled. 'Do you take me for an *am ha'aretz*? Why, I attend a weekly *shiur* by Reb Shlomo Zalman Auerbach!'"

"I apologized, attempting to mollify the man, and then I beat a hasty retreat. I think it would mean a lot to this fellow if the Rav would pay him a brief visit."

Reb Shlomo Zalman followed his escort through the wards until they arrived at the room of the injured party. But his bed was empty. The two men looked at one another in perplexity, until a neighboring patient volunteered that the man had just been released.

The two thanked the informant for the update and hurried out of the hospital. As they neared the doors, Reb Michel offered to call a taxi for the Gaon, but Reb Shlomo Zalman declined. He sent Reb Michel on his way, saying he could manage on his own, and then stepped over to a pay phone to glance at the telephone directory.

Two weeks later Reb Michel happened to notice that very same ex-patient on a bus. He told him that on that fateful Friday, he'd missed a visit from a very distinguished individual.

"Oh, no, I didn't," the man retorted. With obvious pride he recalled how forty minutes before Shabbos, Reb Shlomo Zalman Auerbach, *bi'chvodo uv'atzmo*, had arrived at his house to visit him, apologizing profusely that he hadn't managed to catch him in the hospital.

With an Open Mind and a Warm Heart

A ROSH YESHIVAH POURED his heart out to Reb Shlomo Zalman. His children were far from being the greatest source of *nachas*, he lamented. In fact, they were far, *very* far from even the well-mannered, studious children of his neighbor, who was a simple, unlettered Jew. "How could this have happened?" he implored. "My boys were raised in an atmosphere of Torah!"

Reb Shlomo Zalman explained, "Your children grew up in a home where they may have heard critical remarks made thoughtlessly about the lectures, ideas, and deeds of others who you felt should know better or should have learned better. Your simple neighbor, on the other hand, has only the highest regard for those who are wiser and more learned than he is. He does not view himself as a competitor in any way to those engaged in disseminating Torah. His children saw and heard only respect for scholarship. The end results should therefore be no surprise."

Israel's chief Rabbi, Rav Yisrael Meir Lau, relates that Reb Shlomo Zalman had a great interest in the world at large, aside from Torah learning. For example, once he rode together with the Gaon on a bus which was filled with college students reviewing material for a physics exam. Reb Shlomo Zalman craned his neck to try to overhear their discussions, in the hope of picking up a little something that was previously unknown to him.

Reb Shlomo Zalman read Rabbi Shlomo Rottenberg's *Toldos Am Olam* and took a particular liking to this monumental series on Jewish history. He admired that it was written in a moderate, normal way, without attempting to interject personal views or irrelevant indoctrination.

❀ ❀ ❀

Reb Shlomo Zalman was not only open-minded, but equally tolerant of others. There was no mistaking his perspective and the values he cherished, yet he was not quick to disqualify differing views. When Rav Aharon Lichtenstein, *Rosh Yeshivah* of the *Hesder* yeshiva in Gush Etzion, visited Reb Shlomo Zalman for the first time in 1962, the Gaon asked him what he did for a living. At the time, Rabbi Lichtenstein was teaching English Literature at Yeshiva University. Reb Shlomo Zalman did not bat an eyelash when he heard this, and afforded him the honor due him.

❀❀❀

Rabbi Lau also relates that Reb Shlomo Zalman maintained that a person must employ for the Almighty's sake whatever talent he possesses. The Gaon, basing his opinion on examples from the *Tanach*, considered failure to utilize one's talents not only a sinful waste, but felonious. "One does not have the right to withhold from society the God-given endowments with which he is blessed," he averred. "And furthermore, one should not be ashamed to request more gifts from God."

To support this opinion he cited Leah, who thanked God for the children she had borne. The verse immediately follows with: ותעמוד מלדת — "Then she stopped giving birth." In other words, she should not have been satisfied merely with the blessings she had already received; she should have desired and demanded even more (see Tractate *Berachos* 50).

❃ ❃ ❃

Reb Shlomo Zalman had a deep and abiding love for Eretz Yisrael and especially for Jerusalem — in its figurative and literal sense. He was a true *Yerushalmi* with passionate, unseverable ties to the city in which he was born and raised and where he lived his entire life.

The Gaon held that one should not react with an immediate "Mazal Tov" upon the breaking of the glass under the wedding canopy. Indeed he could not comprehend how people had become accustomed to instantaneously crying "Mazal Tov!" in conjuction with an act performed in commemoration of the destruction of the Temple.

He maintained that it was appropriate to pause and reflect on the destruction, after which a wish of "Mazal Tov" was appropriate to encourage the couple and not allow them to dwell upon sadness at their moment of joy.

At wedding ceremonies, when the glass was broken under the *chuppah*, Reb Shlomo Zalman would recite the verse from Psalms: "If I forget thee, O Jerusalem, may my right hand forget its cunning. May my tongue cleave to my palate if I do not remember you, or set Jerusalem above my greatest joy."

❊ ❊ ❊

On the eve of the Gulf War, when people were fleeing Israel in droves, Reb Shlomo Zalman stated adamantly that one was forbidden to travel abroad and abandon Eretz Yisrael at that trying and stressful time, unless, of course, one's parents insisted.

The Gaon's joy at the overt miracles that were wrought during the war knew no bounds. He declared that if the *Anshei Knesses Ha-Gedolah* were alive today, they would undoubtedly write a sixth *megillah* recording all the wonders and miracles which the Almighty performed on behalf of our People during the war.

❊ ❊ ❊

Reb Shlomo Zalman once received a question regarding the will of Rav Yehudah He-Chasid which stipulates that neither the groom and his prospective father-in-law, nor the bride and her prospective mother-in-law, should bear the same name. The specific instance under discussion was that of a couple who had already begun dating and the relationship had progressed before either side became aware of Rav Yehudah He-Chasid's restrictions.

Reb Shlomo Zalman ruled that the match should be terminated and the will of Rav Yehudah He-Chasid upheld. A few weeks later, however, when the very same question arose concerning a different couple, the Gaon permitted the match to continue.

Those aware of the apparent contradiction were understandably perplexed, until the Rav offered his explanation. "The latter *she'elah* concerned a girl of thirty-two and a boy of thirty-six. Did you see her mother?" the Gaon asked. "The poor woman was on the verge of tears over her daughter's plight!" At thirty-two the girl's marriage prospects were limited, and now that she had at last found a suitable mate, her hopes were threatening to be dashed — over a custom that was from neither the Torah nor the Rabbis.

"However," Reb Shlomo Zalman continued, "the former case concerned a young couple with ample opportunity to find a different

With Reb Chaim Yitzchak Cohen, שליט״א a close confidant and gabbai tzedakah, and Harav Dovid Lifshitz, זצ״ל.

Discussing an issue with Harav Eliezer Mann Shach, שליט״א.

With his brother-in-law, Reb Shlomo Schwadron, "the Maggid of Yerushalayim", שליט״א.

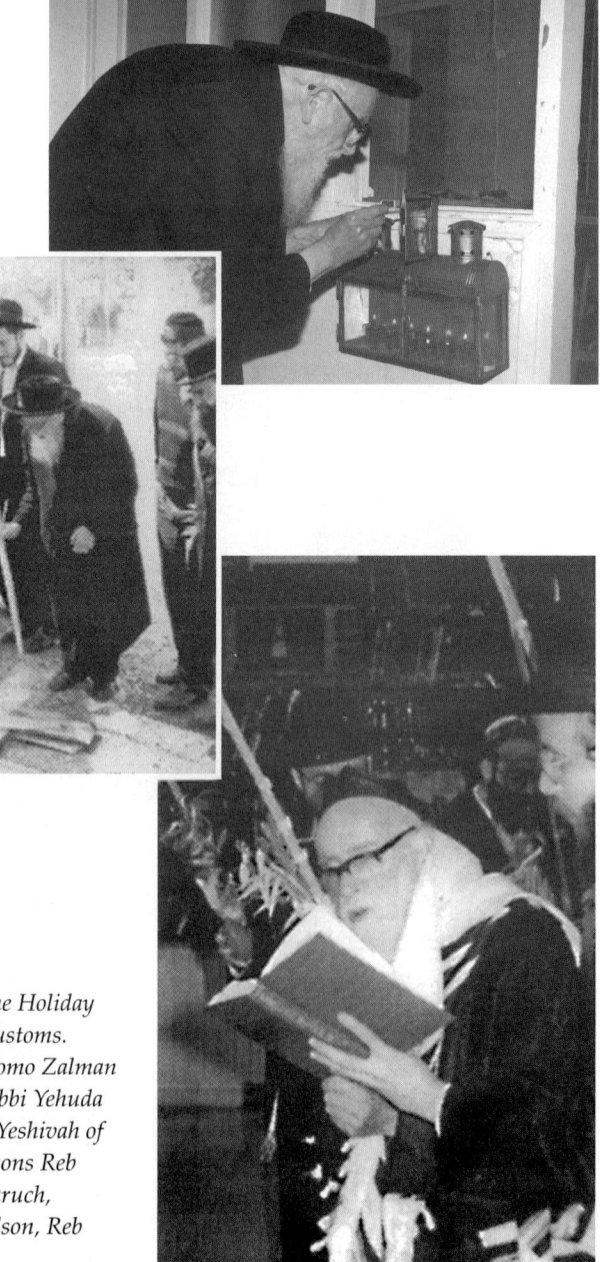

The Gaon observing the Holiday commandments and customs. Pictured with Reb Shlomo Zalman at Bi'ur Chametz: *Rabbi Yehuda Trager,* שליט״א, *Rosh Yeshivah of Antwerp; the Gaon's sons Reb Mordechai and Reb Baruch,* שליט״א, *and his grandson, Reb Aaron Goldberg.*

With Harav Chayim Kanievsky, שליט״א.

With Reb Levi Yitzchak Horowitz, the Bostoner Rebbe, שליט״א.

With (l. to r.) Rabbis Chaim Pinchas Scheinberg; Shmuel Auerbach, Avraham Yosef Laizerzon (speaking); Chaim Kreisworth, Yitzchak Kolitz; and Tzvi Markovitz, Rosh Yeshivah of Karlin-Stolin; Yehudah Adass, Rosh Yeshivah of Kol Yaakov, שליט״א.

Reb Shlomo Zalman casts his ballot in local elections.

At a demonstration opposing construction of the Mormon theological center in Jerusalem. Among those pictured with Reb Shlomo Zalman: Rabbis Shalom Noach Barzevsky, the Slonimer Rebbe; Pinchas Menachem Alter, the Gerrer Rebbe; Simcha Zissel Broyde, Rosh Yeshivah of Chevron; Baruch Shimon Schneerson, Rosh Yeshivah of Tchabin; Avraham Yosef Laizerzon, שליט"א; and Rabbis Shia Brim, Rosh Yeshivah of Bianne; and Simcha Bunim Klein, זצ"ל.

Reb Shlomo Zalman reciting a blessing under the chuppah at the wedding of Reb Zvi Geffen, son-in-law of Rabbi Avigdor Nebanzahl, שליט״א, 1980. Pictured at extreme right: Rabbi Berel Soloveitchik, זצ״ל.

With his son-in-law, Rabbi Zalman Nechemiah Goldberg, שליט״א.

With the Sadigora Rebbe (l.) and the Bianner Rebbe, שליט"א.

With Rabbis Menachem Porush and
Avraham Yosef Laizerzon, שליט"א.

With the groom, at
Reb Chizkiyahu Nebanzahl's wedding.

With Rav Gedalia Eiseman, שליט״א, Mashgiach Emeritus of Kol Torah.

With Rav Mordechai Eliyahu, שליט״א, former Sephardic Chief Rabbi of Israel. Reb Shlomo Zalman's grandson, Rabbi Shimon Trager, שליט״א, is pictured at center.

A tiny fraction of the throngs that gathered to pay their final tribute to the Gaon and brought the city of Jerusalem to a standstill.

Rabbi Yehoshua Y. Neuwirth, שליט״א, comforting the bereaved Auerbach family. Pictured (r. to l.): Reb Ya'akov, Rav and Rosh Kollel of Emanuel; Reb Meir Simcha, Rosh Kollel of Emanuel; Reb Berel, Rosh Yeshivah of Ohr Sameyach; Reb Shmuel, Rosh Yeshivah of Ma'alos Ha-Torah; Reb Avraham Dov, Rav and Rosh Kollel of Tiberias; Reb Ezriel, Rav and Rosh Kollel of Chanichei Ha-Yeshivos.

match. With the older couple I saw significant justification for leniency."

Although a solution to this dilemma is often the addition of an extra name, Reb Shlomo Zalman, in these two instances, apparently deemed this inappropriate.

❈ ❈ ❈

Reb Shlomo Zalman assumed the responsibility for rearing an orphan who lived in his neighborhood. Even as the boy grew to manhood, the Rav did not discard the mantle of accountability for him. Indeed, the Gaon was intimately involved in bringing his ward to the wedding canopy.

When the boy was dating, he spoke to Reb Shlomo Zalman about the dilemma with which he was grappling. The relationship was getting serious and the girl's family had opened negotiations over the financial arrangements. As it turned out, the boy continued, he was short quite a bit from what her family held to be his share of the wedding expenses. He was reluctant to reveal to the Rav the astronomical sum they were demanding.

Reb Shlomo Zalman interrupted the troubled young man to apprise him of some good news. "If you are already speaking about money," he said, improvising, "you should know that I have been overseeing a fund all these years on your behalf. This fund now totals $5,500."

The boy could not believe his ears. Not only was this "fund" a windfall, a fund he had been unaware of until now, but the amount of money in the account was *precisely* the sum that he was missing! This young man had never divulged to anyone, including his benevolent "foster father," the figure that he was expected to provide!

And the benevolent foster father never divulged the fact that until the day of that conversation the "fund" was nonexistent.

Reb Shlomo Zalman did not absolve himself of responsibility for his ward even after the boy was married. He continued to take interest in the boy's development and well-being. When the Rav learned that he was not arising early in the morning as a good Jew should, he tackled the issue head-on.

With the warmth and fatherly concern he had displayed throughout their relationship, the Rav sat the young man down for a heart-to-heart talk. The Gaon revealed that he too had a hard time getting up in the morning, craving the relaxed and leisurely feeling of remaining in bed an extra hour each day. "But I understand the value of order, and you should too. This knowledge compels me to lead my life in an orderly way, which begins with establishing a set time to wake up every morning." The young man could not but comply with the Gaon's wishes.

When Rabbi Mordechai Eilon, *Rosh Yeshivah* of Chorev, came home late one night, he received a message to call Reb Shlomo Zalman urgently, at any hour of the day or night. Despite the urgency of the message, however, Rav Eilon felt it was an indecent hour to disturb the Gaon, and after some deliberation reluctantly delayed phoning until the next morning.

Directly after services, he called Reb Shlomo Zalman, but to his surprise the Gaon put him off, saying, "We will talk later in the day, after you have delivered your lesson." This was certainly not what Rav Eilon had expected to hear about a matter of apparent urgency, perhaps even a life-threatening situation.

The two met later that day and Reb Shlomo Zalman related that the grandfather of a student in Rav Eilon's yeshiva had come to see him and had poured his heart out, saying that he wished his grandson would transfer to a yeshiva where the curriculum was devoted exclusively to Torah study. "I told the grandfather that I would see what I could do about the situation," the Gaon said.

Rabbi Eilon was happy to be of help. "If this is what the Rav wants, then I will gladly..."

But Reb Shlomo Zalman cut him off in mid-sentence. "The issue is not what *I* want," he said. "I am merely conveying the desires of the grandfather. You are the boy's teacher and you are guiding his Torah future. Only you can assess what is best for him."

Rabbi Eilon knew what he had to do, but he had yet to grasp the meaning of the mixed signals he was receiving about the urgency of the matter. "What was so pressing," he inquired, "that the Rav should ask me to call even in the middle of the night?"

Reb Shlomo Zalman explained: "When the grandfather told me that he was so distressed over this that he hadn't been able to sleep for three weeks, I thought to myself, If he hasn't slept for three weeks, what right do I have to sleep?"

❋ ❋ ❋

The Goldbergs were a childless couple who eagerly sought to adopt a Jewish baby. This is by no means a facile undertaking and it becomes well-nigh impossible when the couple in question are Americans, the child Israeli, and the plan is to take the baby abroad. Yet when the call came to the Goldberg home informing them of the availability of a newborn whose mother wished to give him up for adoption, the Goldbergs grabbed the next plane to Israel.

The bris was an extraordinarily joyous occasion not only for the Goldbergs, who were finally able to hold their own child in their arms, but also for all of their friends and relatives who had commiserated with their difficult plight all those years. The Goldbergs rejoiced; they were virtually walking on air.

But then all at once their hopes and dreams were bitterly dashed when they discovered that due to legal complications, under no circumstances would they be able to leave the country with their child.

The Goldbergs were heartbroken and emotionally shattered. Where would they turn for help? They needed a miracle worker.

Mr. Goldberg went to see Reb Shlomo Zalman. Although he had never met the Gaon before, he felt an immediate rapport. It was as though he had known Reb Shlomo Zalman all his life, and the Gaon genuinely understood their travail. Reb Shlomo Zalman listened and commiserated, and then offered this advice: "Wait three months," he said. "In the meantime, place the baby temporarily with a good family and if the matter can be resolved, you'll be able to return to Israel and take your baby back home with you."

Reb Shlomo Zalman never actually came out and said in so many words that he would be the Goldbergs' "father" from then on, but it was understood nevertheless.

For the emotionally charged flight back, with babies seemingly cradled or crawling everywhere on the plane, the Goldbergs' only consolation was the Rav's gentle assurance that all would turn out for the best.

Three months seemed an eternity to wait and Mr. Goldberg found that he was unable to patiently sit it out. After six weeks he called up the temporary foster family, only to learn, amid the woman's sobs and tearful apologies, that the authorities had transferred the baby to the government welfare service.

With a heavy heart Mr. Goldberg informed his wife that the little son whose circumcision they had so happily celebrated was no longer theirs.

Three months to the day after their conversation with Reb Shlomo Zalman, a baby was born and offered for adoption, and this one *was* theirs, with no strings attached. Somehow the Gaon had known what was in store for them and therefore had urged them to wait. The Goldbergs' joy was his joy, and their relationship with their loving "father" only strengthed with each passing year.

❋ ❋ ❋

Letters would arrive at the Auerbach home from all over the world. Some contained queries about the most complex halachic issues affecting entire communities, and some were of a private, personal nature. All received a prompt reply.

One day, among the usual batch of queries and inquiries, requests for blessings and for charitable support, there was a brief letter from a young child. The nine-year-old had written to ask the Gaon to explain a specific *Tosafos*. The little boy had not posed any particular difficulty that was not discussed by the usual commentators, nor had he requested the Gaon's special insight into this commentary. He just wanted to understand what the *Tosafos* said.

Needless to say, there were plenty — including the child's teacher — who could have told the boy the meaning, but Reb Shlomo Zalman took pen in hand to fulfill his correspondent's request. What he wrote was not simply the explanation, but the explanation for a nine-year-old, in a language and style that the budding scholar could comprehend.

❊ ❊ ❊

Once, in the middle of a *shiur*, a student began photographing Reb Shlomo Zalman. Reb Shlomo Zalman was not even aware until the camera had flashed several times. When he realized what was happening, he cracked, "Had you told me in advance, I would have worn my Shabbos suit."

Who Wants to Know?

PART OF Reb Shlomo Zalman's perspicacity lay in his concern with not only the question but the questioner as well, and in his determination to solve in its entirety each problem that was raised. For example, if someone came to him with a question about the permissibility of growing grapes in a particular manner during the *shemittah* year, Reb Shlomo Zalman would delve deeply into the subject until he had a thorough grasp of it and had examined it from every angle. Then he would get well acquainted with the person inquiring about the subject. Finally, he would give his reasoned reply. He was not content to simply answer *muttar* — "permitted," or *assur* — "forbidden"; he was concerned about what would happen with the grapes in all of Eretz Yisrael during the Sabbatical year.

The Rav often complained that people seemed to want to hear the word *assur*, that something was forbidden. But certain technological and other developments, and increased understanding of the world, have rendered things permissible that were once considered *assur*. The challenge was to apply the Halachah to existing circumstances, regardless of their complexity, and to contemporary conditions.

❊ ❊ ❊

A student found he was able to supplement his yeshiva stipend by playing the clarinet at simchas. He came to Reb Shlomo Zalman to ask if it was permissible for him to perform with a band at a wedding in the Bayit Vegan neighborhood of Jerusalem.

At the heart of his question was the over-one-hundred-year-old ruling of the great Rabbis of Jerusalem, which banned musical accompaniment of any instrument but a drum at weddings held in Jerusalem. Realizing that the relatively new neighborhood of Bayit Vegan, located some distance from the Old City, had not existed at the time that the ruling was issued, he felt that there were grounds for leniency.

The Rav answered the young man in a brief Yiddish expression which is generally known, but the student looked puzzled. "Do you know what *zei gezunt* means?" Reb Shlomo Zalman asked him. When the boy nodded, the Gaon turned and went about his business, and the amazed young man realized that his question had been answered. (*Zei gezunt* literally means "Be well" and implies approval.)

When I posed a similar question to Reb Shlomo Zalman prior to my own wedding, I received not one answer, but two. I inquired whether I might hire a band for the affair, and the Rav, recognizing my interest in understanding the subject, took the opportunity to explain that the Rabbis' ruling had not, as many believe, been issued in conjunction with mourning over Jerusalem and a desire to subdue rejoicing in the Holy City in rememberance of the destruction of the Temple and the catastrophe which had befallen our people. Rather, the Sages of then, having witnessed behavior inappropriate for a Jewish wedding, attributed the unruly comportment of the guests to the loud, lively music which accompanied the traditional dancing. Since it is a mitzva to rejoice with a bride and groom, the Rabbis would not forbid music at a wedding altogether, but by limiting the musical accompaniment to only a drum they hoped to prevent unseemly behavior.

The ruling, Reb Shlomo Zalman continued, was not universally accepted and was not likely to apply to a couple from abroad, for example, who are accustomed to having a several-piece band perform at weddings. The issue, then, was not a prohibition, but rather the custom adopted *b'nei Torah* to avoid contravening the ruling.

"However," Reb Shlomo Zalman added, returning to the questioner as he always did, "if, as you say, having a band is important to your *kallah*, there is ample room to be lenient."

I thanked the Gaon and headed down the stairs of his house, when all of a sudden I heard him running after me. He beckoned me to return.

"You told me," he said, "that your fiancée is a descendant of Reb Hirsh Michel Shapiro, may the memory of this *tzaddik* be for a blessing.

That is the finest *yichus* in all of Jerusalem — and he was a party to, if not in fact an initiator of, the ruling. You can hardly have a wedding for the family of Reb Hirsh Michel at which his ban is being violated! The relatives will get upset and turn your simcha into strife. *You* should observe this ban."

✽ ✽ ✽

The day before Reb Shlomo Zalman was to undergo neurosurgery, he called over a *talmid chacham* who lived in the neighborhood. "These lenient dispensations," the Rav said, showing him several responsa he had written on crucial issues, "are my genuine beliefs. I do not know what will happen to me tomorrow or how I will emerge from the operation, so I want you to know: If anyone ever questions what my opinion was and is, I wrote these when I was of sound mind and body, and these are my convictions."

Others in the Gaon's position, confronting a life-threatening situation as he was, tend to act quite differently. They might suddenly become far stricter in their rulings, feeling perhaps unsure of their former leniencies. But this was not the path Reb Shlomo Zalman chose to follow, and his approach was certainly in line with his typical sterling conduct, as these next stories illustrate:

The issue of abortion is a complex and delicate one, but the Halachah addresses the subject forthrightly. It takes a great *Posek*, however, to apply the Halachah to the specific circumstances of each case.

When a particular woman came to Reb Shlomo Zalman to seek his permission to have an abortion, he listened to her detailed presentation, asked a number of pertinent questions, and then ruled in favor of terminating her pregnancy.

That night, the Rav was unable to sleep. He related to a colleague that if a case such as this one were to come to him again, he would carefully think the matter through, and would probably issue the same halachic decision. "And then," he said, "I would *also* have a sleepless night.

"What I cannot comprehend is how those who *forbid* an abortion in these circumstances can sleep so peacefully!"

❈ ❈ ❈

The God-fearing Dr. Falk Schlessinger, a former head of Shaare Zedek Hospital, whom Reb Shlomo Zalman awarded the title *Morenu*, once approached the Gaon with a very difficult halachic question. The following day the Gaon told the doctor that his question was so perplexing that he had been unable to sleep all night.

The well-bred physician, whose manner reflected his refined Germanic unbringing, apologized profusely for having caused the Rav discomfort and begged his forgiveness for disturbing his slumber. Reb Shlomo Zalman dismissed Dr. Schlessinger's concern with a smile. "Your job is to ask," the Gaon replied. "My job is not to be able to fall asleep."

❀ ❀ ❀

A wealthy individual who apparently held himself in high esteem came to visit Reb Shlomo Zalman. The philanthropist, immaculately attired, addressed the Gaon in a manner that matched his sartorial splendor.

"You are a highly respected personage," he said by way of greeting. "It is therefore beyond my comprehension that you should involve yourself with the multitude of intricacies relevant to the subject of infertility. It is simply inappropriate for an individual of your stature."

Reb Shlomo Zalman asked his guest to clarify his objection. The Rav assumed that his distinguished detractor wished to challenge the halachic validity of his numerous dispensations, and would attempt to prove that they were not halachically sound.

But this man's objections lay neither in the realm of Torah nor in medical expertise. Rather, he felt that it was undignified for a *talmid chacham* of Reb Shlomo Zalman's standing to concern himself with an issue relating to *women*.

After hearing the nature of the objection, Reb Shlomo Zalman asked this individual how many children he had.

"Six," he replied proudly.

"Are you not ashamed of yourself?" the Gaon demanded. "You and your wife have, thank God, six children, while there are many couples who have none. May you never know suffering like that of these couples whose anguish is so great and whose misery so keen. I see nothing inappropriate about dealing with their plight, and, with God's help, perhaps relieving it. The subject is too vital to be left only to others. For me it is both a duty and an honor."

He Caused the Widow's Heart to Sing

IN SHAAREI CHESED there lived an elderly widow who earned her meager livelihood from selling wines. Probably unable to distinguish between a Dry and a Semi-dry, and certainly not between a Chardonnay and a Cabernet, she had not chosen this profession, but rather had inherited the modest enterprise from her late husband.

Every *erev Pesach*, after *bedikas chametz*, Reb Shlomo Zalman would trek to this woman's "store" — that is, to her house — to buy wine for Pesach. He was particular to make the purchases himself, and never sent an emissary wine-shopping on his behalf. In truth he had no need for the wine, for there were always enough bottles in his house from the many packages of *mishlo'ach manos* he would receive on Purim, enough to last for an entire year, and most of that wine was kosher for Pesach.

As time went by, and this widow became advanced in years, she was no longer able to maintain her business, and eventually she closed her "store." However, on *erev Pesach* she instructed one of her grandchildren to buy the type of wine that Reb Shlomo Zalman would always purchase, along with a few other bottles, so that the former wine department of her home would still have the ambience of a liquor store. She had always welcomed the Gaon's annual visits, as well as his patronage, and didn't want him to stop coming when he found the business had closed.

Reb Shlomo Zalman was wise to her little deception, but he never let on. He continued to make his modest purchases, thanking the woman profusely each time for enabling him to prepare for the Seder.

❋ ❋ ❋

One *erev Pesach* an eldery widow approached Reb Shlomo Zalman with a practical *she'elah*. She explained that the Romaine lettuce she had bought for the Seder was full of bugs, but her eyesight was no longer good enough for her to inspect the leaves properly. What should she do?

Reb Shlomo Zalman instructed her to bring her lettuce to him so that he could take a look at it for her. Possibly he had not anticipated the inordinately large number of lettuce leaves the widow had in her possession; nonetheless, he examined each and every one. The job took the Gaon two solid hours, standing outside in the sun, and when it was done he returned the bug-free greens to their grateful owner.

❋ ❋ ❋

For many years, the local grocery store in Reb Shlomo Zalman's neighborhood was run by a widow. To operate such a store from early in the morning until late in the evening consumed every ounce of the poor woman's strength. Delivery vans would pull up at the crack of dawn, and the truckers would deposit the crates of milk and dairy products on the sidewalk. Later, the widow would drag them inside herself when she opened the store. One day, to her great delight, she saw that the crates, instead of being stacked all the way across the sidewalk, had been placed right at the front entrance, making her workload infinitely lighter.

This phenomenon recurred the following morning, and continued on a daily basis. The widow felt that she had to thank the drivers personally for this tremendous favor, so she made a point of arriving at the store very early one morning to await the deliveries. However, to her amazement, when the vans appeared the men deposited her crates on the edge of the sidewalk as they always had in the past.

Perplexed, she stood on the pavement wondering how the dairy products had transported themselves to her door, when suddenly the figure of Reb Shlomo Zalman Auerbach appeared, *tallis* bag under his arm. One by one, he lifted the heavy crates and deposited them in front of the grocery store, and then he hurried off to shul.

Rebbetzin Herzog enjoyed a vibrant, exciting life, with the house always full of people, as long as her husband was alive. But with the passing of Rabbi Isaac Herzog, Chief Rabbi of Israel, the spark of the Rebbetzin's active communal life went out. Gone were the days when *Gedolim* and prominent community leaders would come to call. As time went by few even bothered to inquire after her well-being. Reb Shlomo Zalman Auerbach was a noteworthy exception. Every *Chol Ha-Mo'ed*, both Pesach and Sukkos, he came to give her holiday greetings and wish her well.

❊ ❊ ❊

Time of course was Reb Shlomo Zalman's greatest commodity: the commodity which he valued most and with which he was the most generous. Since his time for learning was at a premium, he rented a small room in Shaarei Chesed where he was able to study without interruption.

Reb Shlomo Zalman's landlady for this secluded *beis midrash* was an aged widow who lived across the courtyard from the rented room. A meticulous housekeeper, the widow spent a good part of her day airing linens, hanging laundry, and washing floors, including the paving stones of the courtyard.

If, when the Gaon neared the house, he happened to see this woman washing the courtyard, he would quickly turn around before she noticed him and wait in the street until he was certain that the paving stones were dry. Every second of learning was precious to him, but the feelings of a widow were more precious still.

When someone brought to Reb Shlomo Zalman's attention the plight of a particular widow, the Rav took immediate action. She desperately needed financial assistance for an urgent medical procedure. Time was of the essence, but to have the operation performed right away with a top-flight surgical team would require a lot of money, and Reb Shlomo Zalman's charitable resources were all but depleted.

He summoned Reb Dovid Goldwicht, one of his key assistants in philanthropic matters, to help him launch a door-to-door fundraising campaign. "...You will start on this side of the street," the Gaon said, "and I will start on the other side, and please God by the time we meet, we will have raised the necessary sum."

the Widow's Heart / 367

The two did in fact meet somewhere midway in the neighborhood, but "midway" was clearly the operative word: although they had visited every household in the community, they had raised only half the amount of money that was required.

Reb Shlomo Zalman was undaunted. The health of the poor widow was at stake and there was no time left for an additional, wider-ranging appeal. Something had to be done now and there was only one man who could do it: Reb Shlomo Zalman Auerbach himself.

The Gaon traveled to Hadassah Hospital to meet with the surgeon in person and have a heart-to-heart talk. The physician, a professor at the Medical School, was the foremost in the country in his field, and had the arrogant bearing of a man who knew it. By all accounts, his skill in the operating theater was matchless, and thus he could demand and receive an exorbitant, non-negotiable fee for his services.

Since their patients are usually sedated or unconscious, surgeons do not always cultivate a warm bedside manner, and this surgeon was one of the chillier members of that profession. Not (yet) religious himself, he was especially apathetic to Orthodox patients and their problems, and even more so to the overtly religious man who had abruptly barged into his office unannounced.

The intervention of a medical secretary had earned Reb Shlomo Zalman a few moments of the doctor's precious time, long enough for the Gaon to get the measure of the man. As sometimes is the case with medical practitioners, the surgeon was brilliant with a scalpel but had long since forgotten Who guided his hand. During the brief audience Reb Shlomo Zalman had been granted, the doctor glanced repeatedly at his watch, but the Rav was unimpressed.

With complete candor, Reb Shlomo Zalman told the professor the truth, that he and his colleague had worked feverishly to raise the funds necessary for the widow's operation, yet despite their arduous efforts had succeeded in raising only half the fee. "I wish therefore to make you a proposition," the Rav ventured. "Let's split this mitzva evenly between us."

The silence in the well-appointed office was palpable as the doctor blinked and gaped over the audacious proposal. Then he thrust out his hand and the deal was struck. Several hours later, the widow underwent life-saving surgery.

❊ ❊ ❊

The young widow who entered Reb Shlomo Zalman's study had a lot on her mind. She availed herself of the Gaon's warm demeanor to unburden herself, while he, as ever, listened with patience and sensitivity. First, there was her own predicament, which was lonely and painful, but this of course paled alongside the situation of her four fatherless children. Most troublesome of all were the relentlessly recurring pangs of conscience she experienced, urging her to perform a positive act of spiritual self-improvement, which would uplift the soul of her husband.

Reb Shlomo Zalman instructed her to listen very carefully to what he was about to say. "I understand your need to do a *tikkun* for an *illui neshamah* for your departed husband. This is surely a blessed and worthy desire," the Gaon told her. "Now, go out and buy toys and games for the children. A lot of them! Then take the children out for walks and outings; this will be the very best *illui neshamah* for your husband! Forget your mourning and concentrate on making the children rejoice and enjoy life."

A Time for Joy,
A Time for Grief

SEVENTY-TWO HOURS can seem like an eternity when one is awaiting glad tidings. Seventy-two hours is more than enough time to prepare oneself for joy. But for sad news, seventy-two hours is not nearly sufficient; it passes like a tiny fragment of a fraction of a second. The thought that someone so dear could suddenly be gone — that thought can barely reach the information processing center of the brain in seventy-two hours, let alone penetrate the heart. The emotional barriers which block the passage of such terrible messages are too formidable to be breached in so short a span of time.

Seventy-two hours — three short days — was all Reb Shlomo Zalman had to absorb that terrible message about his beloved Rebbetzin, his *eishes ne'urim* who had served as partner and helpmate for over fifty years. Thursday night she felt unwell; Shabbos she was gone. At the *seudah shelishis* the Auerbachs' eldest son, Reb Shmuel — the *Rosh Yeshivah* of Ma'alos Ha-Torah — began to weep, and his father admonished him for allowing his sorrow to desecrate the holy Sabbath.

When the Sabbath Queen had departed, Reb Shlomo Zalman's own sorrow burst its bounds. He traveled to the hospital to sign the documents and whatever other papers the administrative staff thrust before him, and then made his way to the ward where his Rebbetzin's body still lay. He handed his overcoat to the student who had accompanied him, and then entered the room alone.

His grief was overwhelming, but it was *his* grief, not to be imposed on others. When he emerged from the hospital room, his anguish apparent, the student meekly offered Reb Shlomo Zalman his overcoat, and the Rav accepted it with a gracious smile. As he neared the hospital exit, a former student from the Kol Torah Yeshiva, unaware of the tragic circumstances which had brought the Rav to the hospital, greeted Reb Shlomo Zalman with the good news that his wife had just given birth to a baby boy. Again Reb Shlomo Zalman detached himself from his personal agony and showered the young father with blessings.

If behaving with *derech eretz* even in a moment of intense *tza'ar* presented a challenge to Reb Shlomo Zalman, there was no evidence of it. On the contrary, expressing gratitude for even the smallest of favors and joy for someone's happy event was as natural for the Rav as breathing. The real challenge of this sorrowful time yet lay ahead.

In the modest home of Reb Shlomo Zalman and his Rebbetzin lived the Rebbetzin's frail and elderly mother. At the age of ninety-six and in so fragile a state of health that whenever she would place her head down to rest the family feared that she would not lift it again, she could hardly be expected to receive the news of her only daughter's demise with equanimity. The consensus among the family members was to conceal the tidings from their grandmother, at least until after the funeral, lest the news alone prove fatal to someone in such delicate condition.

Reb Shlomo Zalman emphatically disagreed. It was the woman's right, he declared, to be informed *before* the funeral and even to attend, if she chose to do so. Furthermore, he would allow no one but himself to accept the awesome responsibility of delivering the news to the Rebbetzin's mother. To do otherwise would be blatantly disrespectful. And with that, he turned toward her room to meet the challenge as only Reb Shlomo Zalman could.

Quietly the Rav entered his mother-in-law's room and gently closed the door. She lifted her eyes to him expectantly and saw the pain engraved on his face. With the utmost respect he said, "You know that the Holy One is good and all that He does is good. Sometimes we understand His ways, and sometimes we do not. You should know that the Almighty in His wisdom has taken your daughter to a place that is entirely good, and now you and I will together recite the blessing of *Dayan Ha-Emmes*, word by word, without crying."

Silence filled the tiny room. Then the elderly woman, whose own life seemed to hang by a tenuous thread, asked in a quavering voice, "How can I say it without crying?"

"All your life you have been a *tzaddekes*," her son-in-law replied. "You are able to accept this trial as well."

Together the grieving mother and husband recited the blessing, word after word, without a tear, affirming their conviction that the Almighty God is the True Judge. By the time Reb Shlomo Zalman rejoined the family in the next room, he was sobbing uncontrollably and near collapse.

❊ ❊ ❊

Later that night, at the funeral, he bade farewell to his life's partner with these inspiring words:

"It is customary to request forgiveness from the deceased. However, I have nothing to ask your forgiveness for. During the course of our relationship, never did anything occur that would require either of us to ask the other's forgiveness. Each of us led our life in accordance with the *Shulchan Aruch*."

This simple truth remains inscribed in the hearts and minds of all who were present on that sorrowful night, an eternal lesson in living a meaningful, Torah-true existence.

A Fitting Farewell

S THEY LOOK BACK, members of the family, as well as the physicians who attended him, cannot help but be confounded by the amazing series of events that accompanied the deterioration of Reb Shlomo Zalman's medical condition up until his demise. There were many indications that the end was drawing near, but after He sealed the decree, the Master of the Universe worked discreetly, such that even professional eyes would be blinded to the seriousness of his illness.

Below is a chronicle of the Gaon's last five days:

On Wednesday, Reb Shlomo Zalman attended the bris of the son of his faithful assistant, Reb Chayim Suisa. When the Rav arrived, he learned that the *mohel* was unwilling to perform the circumcision because the baby was jaundiced. Reb Shlomo Zalman asked if there was a doctor present, and as it happened, there was in fact a pediatrician among the guests. He examined the infant and, on the basis of his findings, Reb Shlomo Zalman ruled that the circumcision could proceed.

After the ceremony, the Gaon congratulated and blessed the father, and then left for home with his grandson, Reb Shimon Trager. When the car pulled up at the Auerbach home, Reb Shimon quickly climbed out and went around to open the door on Reb Shlomo Zalman's side. The Rav stared at the door a moment and said, "I don't have the strength to get out. I have a pain on the right side of my chest."

Reb Shimon returned to the driver's seat and conversed with his frail grandfather for a few minutes, and then asked if he was ready to get out yet. "I still don't have the strength," Reb Shlomo Zalman answered.

A Fitting Farewell / 377

Some time later, the Rav agreed to allow Reb Shimon to lift his feet out of the car and help him alight and climb the stairs to his house. Arm in arm, they slowly crossed the pavement. As they drew close to the house, Reb Shlomo Zalman noticed a small crowd of people who had come to speak with him and seek his advice. He gestured to them to wait. Inside, he turned to Reb Shimon and said, "Please ask that only those with pressing problems come in."

While Reb Shlomo Zalman had been sitting in the car trying to summon the strength to get out, the members of his family were becoming increasingly worried, wondering why the Rav had not yet returned. Reb Shmuel Auerbach phoned all his brothers and sisters to ask if perhaps their father had gone to one of them, but none of them knew their father's whereabouts.

When Reb Shimon entered supporting the Rav, Reb Shmuel rushed to his father's side and asked anxiously, "What happened? What took so long?"

Reb Shimon explained that his grandfather was not feeling well, but Reb Shlomo Zalman waved his son away, declaring, "Everything is all right." Reb Shmuel could see that everything was *not* all right. He asked the people waiting outside to leave. "The rabbi is not feeling well and cannot see anyone," he said.

The Gaon, never one to turn away a visitor, insisted that the people be allowed to enter.

"They've gone," Reb Shmuel told him, coming back into the house.

The Rav was dismayed. "They've gone?" he repeated. "Please go and check," he told Reb Shimon. "Perhaps there is still someone remaining."

Reb Shimon did as his grandfather requested, and returned to report that there was no one waiting outside.

"How can it be that everyone left?" Reb Shlomo Zalman asked, puzzled. "They heard I wasn't feeling well, and they *all left*?"

Reb Shmuel finally confessed that he had told the people that the Rav could not see anyone. Reb Shlomo Zalman stared at his son. "From *my* house, people were driven away?" He was appalled at the notion.

Then began a heated debate over calling a doctor. Reb Shimon wanted to; Reb Shlomo Zalman declared that there was no need. Reb Shimon protested.

"Are you a doctor?" the Rav demanded. "I tell you there is no need."

A few minutes later, however, Reb Shlomo Zalman relented. "Professor Avraham of Shaarei Zedek is coming to speak to me this evening about some other matter," he informed his son. "Please call him and tell him to be sure to bring his instruments."

Prof. Avraham Avraham arrived promptly at five o'clock. The noted physician, cardiology specialist, and author of several books on medical Halachah, examined the Gaon thoroughly and, to everyone's relief, diagnosed a muscle strain and a touch of bronchitis — nothing more. He prescribed an antibiotic. The Almighty, in His infinite wisdom, chose to conceal the Rav's true condition from this brilliant doctor.

Later that evening, the Rav walked to shul for services, stopping along the way to give *tzedakah* to several poor people. He had intended to speak later to Reb Shlomo Zalman

Sonnenfeld, a well-known *gabbai tzedakah* who worked together with the Gaon, about helping out a particular widow. Reb Shlomo Zalman thought that as usual he would walk to the Chasidim Shul in the neighborhood, climb all the stairs, and meet with Rav Sonnenfeld, but someone had the foresight to run ahead and ask Rav Sonnenfeld to come down. Reb Shlomo Zalman wondered how his colleague had known he was coming to see him.

When he returned home, Reb Shlomo Zalman mentioned that his cousin, Reb Mendel Auerbach, was having a חנוכת הבית, a housewarming, that night. Reb Mendel had always been a great help to him, the Rav said, and so to show his appreciation he intended to join him on the happy occasion. Members of the family tried to dissuade their father, reminding him that he had been feeling unwell earlier, but Reb Shlomo Zalman prevailed.

On Thursday morning, as he walked to services, he complained that his foot was hurting him. Rabbi Elimelech Kupperman, who was escorting him, thought that perhaps Reb Shlomo Zalman had tied his shoelace too tightly, and stooped to check. Nothing seemed amiss, so the two continued on their way. They had managed to walk no more than a few steps when the Gaon stumbled. Rabbi

Kupperman managed to catch him before he fell, but he was very concerned. "Perhaps we should go home," he suggested.

The idea of missing the Thursday Torah reading did not appeal to Reb Shlomo Zalman. Instead, he went on to shul and attended the services, although he remained seated throughout, unable to stand for the designated portions. Then again, when he returned home, Reb Shlomo Zalman said he was not feeling well.

Extremely weak, the Gaon sat down at his table in the afternoon and asked his son, Reb Baruch, to bring him his checkbook and the envelopes made out to all those who had requested financial assistance. He told Reb Baruch the amount to fill in for each check and then signed them all, asking Reb Baruch to turn the pages of the checkbook for him as he hadn't the strength to do it himself. He refused to eat lunch until the very last check was written and signed. The members of the family kept all visitors away from the house, but Reb Shlomo Zalman did answer a number of questions over the telephone. For perhaps the first time in his life, he recited the *Minchah* service in bed.

Realizing that their father's condition was deteriorating, the family called another doctor, who examined him and found that he had developed a very mild case of pneumonia. He ordered him hospitalized, just in case, reassuring the family that he would be released in a short time. Reb Shlomo Zalman, however, sensing that he would be gone a lot longer than anyone surmised, insisted on changing to his Shabbos attire before the ambulance came.

Shaarei Chesed is a small neighborhood, and the sight of an ambulance outside the home of the *Posek Ha-dor* quickly attracted a crowd of neighbors. The ambulance attendants helped Reb Shlomo Zalman into a wheelchair and transported him down the stairs. The Gaon waved from the wheelchair and took his leave of his grandchildren.

Once aboard the ambulance, the medic took Reb Shlomo Zalman's blood pressure and pulse. "*K'vod Ha-Rav*," he said, "everything seems to be fine. I don't understand why you need to go to the hospital." The situation was genuinely puzzling.

After X-rays and a preliminary examination in the emergency room, the Rav was admitted to the Department of Internal Medicine. Sharing his room was a young man waiting to be released the following morning, and Reb Shlomo Zalman spoke with him at length.

Relatives who heard of the Gaon's hospitalization rushed to the hospital. Among his visitors was his son-in-law, Rav Zalman Nechemiah Goldberg. "There's nothing you can do for me," Reb Shlomo Zalman said to him. "Why did you come?" Other members of the family were kept at a distance so that the Rav would not become frightened upon seeing that so many of them had arrived.

On Friday morning, Reb Shlomo Zalman laid his *tefillin* and recited *Shacharis*. Then the Rav surprised his family with an instruction to give the woman who cleaned his house 200 shekels. This princely sum was several times the going rate, and although the family did not know exactly how much Reb Shlomo Zalman usually paid the woman, as he had always attended to the matter himself, the figure sounded inordinately high. Upon seeing their querulous expressions, Rav Shlomo Zalman explained that keeping house for him was her livelihood and from this money she sustained herself the entire week. And with that, the subject was closed.

As Reb Shlomo Zalman was experiencing some difficulty breathing, a staff doctor connected him to an oxygen apparatus, but his overall condition remained satisfactory. It was not until around noon on Friday, while asleep, that this generation's mentor in Halachah, diligence, humility, and character had his first heart attack.

With this most recent development, realization finally dawned on one and all that the Gaon's condition was serious. Word spread like wildfire and *Klal Yisrael* was gripped with fear of the impending loss. The religious community, still reeling from the terrible losses it had sustained in recent years, refused to accept this decree. Synagogues immediately filled and the walls reverberated with the intense recitation of *tehillim,* beseeching the Master of the Universe to have mercy on His people, who so sorely needed their leader.

The entire family remained in the hospital over Shabbos and prayed at their father's bedside. When they sang *Yedid Nefesh* to the tune he favored, Reb Shlomo Zalman's entire body trembled at the lyrics.

On Saturday night, the Rav's doctor reported that his condition had stabilized. Nonetheless, sound trucks began to circulate right after *Havdalah* in Bnei Brak and Jerusalem, imploring everyone to pray for the

Gaon's well-being. Thousands flocked to the *Kosel* to join in a massive gathering, and all night long the throngs wept and recited heartfelt *tefillos*, pleading the Gaon's case before the Heavenly Court.

At 9:30 Sunday night, 20 Adar Aleph 5755, with the hospital corridors crammed with swaying worshipers, family members and disciples gathered around Reb Shlomo Zalman to intone the words of *Shema Yisrael* as the heart of the Jewish People's great leader beat its last.

Word of the Gaon's demise shook the country and the entire Diaspora. From all over Israel and abroad former students and colleagues began to arrive and the streets of Jerusalem started to fill with mourners. Jews of every stripe flocked to Shaarei Chesed from where the funeral procession would commence. All of the Rabbinical courts proclaimed a *bittul melachah* and shut down, and every yeshiva in the country followed suit.

When the streets of Shaarei Chesed were filled to capacity, the mourners overflowed into all the adjacent neighborhoods, spreading out from the city center and covering the entire north and west sides of Jerusalem in a sea of humanity. The main highway from Tel Aviv had to be closed at Mevasseret Tziyon, ten kilometers west of Jerusalem, as the traffic at the city's entrance gridlocked. The police estimated a crowd of three hundred thousand; other sources have suggested the number was even greater. Jerusalem had never seen so vast a funeral.

The man who had fled from honor as though fleeing for his very survival; the man who had rejected all titles and honorifics including the one which described him best — *Posek Ha-dor*; the man who had avoided all political activity and received every Jew with sincere warmth and personal concern — his life and works ensured that in death he would receive the honor due the prince and foremost decisor of Halachah in our time. His final wish was that his parting serve as an inspiration for the Jewish People, to awaken in them love of Torah, fear of Heaven, and genuine repentance, and that his family and all of Israel be privileged to serve God in joy. He asked that praise not be heaped upon him, but what higher form of praise exists than the outpouring of sorrow and pain from the heart of world Jewry over the passing of their father!

❊ ❊ ❊

The tribute to Reb Shlomo Zalman was simple and subdued. His brother, Reb Avraham Dov Auerbach, began, addressing the deceased as is customary. "In accordance with your wishes, only two persons will deliver eulogies at your funeral."

Then he read aloud portions of the Gaon's last will and testament.*

"The headstone will be a regular one and will stand no higher than those of my dear parents. You may add to the engraving: העמיד תלמידים בישיבת קול תורה והרביץ תורה לרבים — He nurtured students at Kol Torah Yeshiva and disseminated Torah to the masses.

"If anyone wishes to deliver a eulogy, I ask that it be brief and exclude any words of praise. Let them speak only words of inspiration to love of Torah, fear of Heaven, and improvement of deeds and character.

"I request that my family not ask others to deliver eulogies at the end of the mourning period, but if there are those who wish to, I

---

* This document, called a *tzava'ah*, "will" or "order," was headed *bakashah*, "request," by the Rav.

again request them not to heap praises upon me. Such practices caused me pain during my lifetime, particularly the exaggerations written about me in recent years. I also repeat my request not to speak at length, as this is an imposition on the listeners.

"I grant complete forgiveness to every person, and request of all who feel that I have wronged them, whether intentionally or inadvertently, to be merciful and forgive me.

"If my last years are difficult, I request that I be admitted to a good institution for the aged, for I would not like to be a burden to my family.

"I close with the hope that the Holy One, Who is All-Merciful and Forgiving, Who knows the sorrow of my heart, will have mercy upon me and forgive me for all my sins and violations, for I certainly regret them. I request with all my heart that the Holy One send His blessings to the members of my family, and that you all be privileged to serve Him in joy all your days."

❊ ❊ ❊

He was a child progidy, a son of Shaarei Chesed and Jerusalem's "old Yishuv"; a living link to Sinai through his father, Reb Chaim Yehudah Leib, and his teacher, Reb Isser Zalman Meltzer; he was a master of outstanding character and lovingkindness; a father to *Ge'onim* and *Rashei Yeshivah*; and he was the foremost *Posek* to the first generations to grapple with such technological developments as electricity, computers, and organ transplants, and the unprecedented return of the Jewish People to its Land. His passing created a void that is yet to be filled. Reb Shlomo Zalman Auerbach, may the memory of this great *tzaddik* and loving leader of his nation forever be blessed, has left this fleeting existence to respond to a Higher Calling, but he lives on in the hearts and souls of the People who revered him and in the minds of those who learned his Torah.

The sight of over three hundred thousand mourners paying their last respects to an eighty-four-year-old rabbi whose face had never graced the cover of *Time* or *Newsweek*, caught the secular public very much by surprise. While the broadcast media scrambled frantically to gather information to explain the phenomenon, the "intelligentsia" attempted to quantify it, all to no avail. How can one explain the incisive brilliance of a halachic decision to those unfamiliar with the word *Halachah*?

A young reporter for a secular paper phoned the editor of a religious weekly and told him that he had been allocated a full page for a story on the candidates for the successor to Rabbi Auerbach. "What can you tell me?" the eager journalist asked.

The editor paused to think a moment before responding. "I'm sorry, young man," he finally sighed. "I guess you'll just have to leave your page blank."

Glossary

The following glossary provides a partial explanation of some of the Hebrew, Yiddish, and Aramaic words and phrases used in this book. The spellings and explanations reflect the way the specific word is used herein. Often, there are alternate spellings and meanings for the words. Those foreign words and phrases which have become a part of comtemporary English usage can be found in Webster's and other dictionaries.

ADAM GADOL: a great person.
AVINU: our father.
AVRECH: a married yeshiva student.

BAAL TESHUVAH: a penitent; a formerly non-Observant Jew who returns to Torah observance.

BACHUR: a young man; a yeshiva student.

BAR MITZVA: a Jewish boy of 13, the age at which he assumes religious obligations; the celebration in honor of the occasion.

BEDIKAS CHAMETZ: the search for leaven conducted on the night before Pesach.

BEIS DIN: a court of Jewish law.

BEIS HA-MIKDASH: the Holy Temple in Jerusalem.

BEIS MIDRASH: the study hall of a yeshiva.

BEN (BNEI) TORAH: learned, Observant Jew(s).

BERACHAH (-CHOS): blessing(s).

BERACHAH L'VATALAH: a blessing recited in vain.

BI'CHVODO UV'ATZMO: lit., "his honorable self," that is, in person.

BRIS: the ritual of circumcision; the celebration held in honor of the event.

CHASID(IM): followers of the teachings of the Baal Shem Tov, which stressed purity of heart and serving God with joy.

CHASSAN: a bridegroom.

CHAZAL: the Hebrew acronym for "our Sages, of blessed memory."

CHAZZAN: a cantor; one who leads the prayer services.

CHEDER (Y.): a religious primary school for boys.

CHEDER YICHUD: the room where the newlywed couple spend time alone together after the ceremony.

CHESED: lovingkindness; compassion.

CHEVRUSA (A.): a study partner.

CHIDDUSH: an innovation; a new interpretation in Torah study.

GLOSSARY / 393

CHUPPAH: the wedding canopy; the wedding ceremony.

DAVEN (Y.): to pray.

DAYAN: a judge in a rabbinical court.

DERECH ERETZ: decent behavior; courtesy and consideration.

DREIKUPS (Y.): pests.

EISHES NE'URIM: the wife one married when they were young.

EMMES: truth; certainty.

ERETZ YISRAEL: the Land of Israel.

EREV PESACH: the day preceding Pesach.

GABBAI TZEDAKAH: the treasurer of a charity fund.

GADOL HA-DOR: the greatest Torah authority of the generation.

GAON: a genius.

GEMACH: the Hebrew acronym for "benevolence"; an interest-free loan society.

GEMARA: commentary on the MISHNAH (together they comprise the Talmud).

GEZEL ZEMAN: "stealing" another's time, that is, taking his valuable time unnecessarily.

HAKARAS HA-TOV: gratitude; appreciation.

HALACHAH: the entire body of Jewish Law.

HA-MOTZI: the blessing recited over bread.

HASMADAH: diligence and perseverance in Torah study.

HAVDALAH: the ceremony marking the end of the Sabbath, in which blessings are recited, separating the holy day from the other days of the week.

HECHSHER: authoritative certification that food is kosher.

ISH HA-HALACHAH: lit., "a man of the Law," that is, one who has a total grasp of and promulgates Jewish Law.

KABBALAS SHABBOS: "welcoming the Sabbath," the Friday night prayer service.

KADDISH: the mourner's prayer.

KALLAH: a bride.

KEHILLAH: a Jewish community or congregation.

KIBBUD AV: the mitzva of honoring one's father.

KIDDUSH: sanctification of the Sabbath, usually recited over a cup of wine.

KIDDUSHIN: marriage.

KIRUV RECHOKIM: lit., "bringing the far ones near"; bringing non-Observant Jews closer to Jewish tradition and Torah observance.KLAL YISRAEL: the Jewish People.

KOLLEL: a center for advanced Torah learning for adult students, mostly married men.

KOSEL: the Western Wall, the only extant remnant of the wall which surrounded the courtyard of the BEIS HA-MIKDASH.

K'VOD HA'RAV: "his honor, the Rabbi," a respectful address.

MA'ARIV: the evening prayer service.

MACHMIR: one who interprets the HALACHAH stringently.

MALACH: an angel.

MASECHES: a tractate of the Talmud.

MAZAL TOV: "Congratulations!"

ME'ARAS HA-MACHPELAH: the Cave of the Patriarchs in Hebron.

MECHITZAH: a partition dividing the men's section from the women's section in a synagogue or at a social event.

MECHUTANIM: in-laws; the parents of one's son-in-law or daughter-in-law.

MECHUTENESTE (Y.): the mother of one's son-in-law or daughter-in-law.

MEGILLAH: a scroll; the Scroll of Esther, read on Purim.

MEKEL: one who interprets the HALACHAH leniently.

MELAVEH MALKAH: a Saturday night celebration honoring the departing "Sabbath queen."

MESADER KIDDUSHIN: one who officiates at a wedding ceremony.

MEZONOS: the blessing recited over pastries and baked goods.

MIDDOS TOVOS: positive character traits.

MIKVEH: a pool for ritual immersion.

MINCHAH: the afternoon prayer service.

MINYAN: a minimum of ten Jewish males aged 13 and over, the quorum for communal prayer.

MISHLO'ACH MANOS: [the sending of] Purim delicacies to friends and neighbors.

MISHNAH: an orderly redaction and summary by R. Yehudah Ha-Nasi of the accumulated Oral Law, which forms the basis of the Talmud.

MOHEL: one who performs the ritual of circumcision.

MORENU: "our teacher."

MOTZA'EI SHABBOS: the departure of the Sabbath, Saturday night.

MUSAR: Torah ethics and values.

NACHAS: pleasure; pride; satisfaction.

POSEK: a halachic authority.

POSHETER YID (Y.): a simple Jew.

PSAK: a halachic ruling.

RAM(IM): the Hebrew acronym for "rabbi-teacher," a senior teacher in a yeshiva.

RASHKEBEHAG: the Hebrew acronym for "Rabbi of all world Jewry."

REBBE: a rabbi; a Torah teacher; a Chasidic leader.

REBBETZIN (Y.): the wife of a rabbi.

ROSH YESHIVAH: the dean of a YESHIVA.

SANDEK (Y.): one who has the honor of holding the baby on his lap for the circumcision.

SECHEL: intelligence; common sense.

SEDER (SEDARIM) (1): the order of the Pesach night ceremony recalling the Exodus from Egypt and the liberation from bondage.

SEDER (SEDARIM) (2): study session(s) in a yeshiva.

SEFER (SEFARIM): book(s); holy book(s).

SEMICHAH: rabbinical ordination.

SEUDAH SHELISHIS: the third Sabbath meal.

SEVARA (A.): a logical argument; a deduction; reasoning.

SHACHARIS: the morning prayer service.

SHADCHAN: a matchmaker.

SHALOM BAYIS: marital harmony; domestic tranquillity.

SHAVUA TOV: "Have a good week!", a greeting exchanged on Saturday night after Shabbos.

SHE'ELAH: a question; a halachic question.

SHEMITTAH: the Sabbatical year.

SHEMONEH ESREH: the Eighteen Benedictions, or *Amidah* prayer.

SHIDDUCH: a marital match.

SHINUI HA-SHEM: [the ceremony for] changing a person's name, specifically in order to spare the life of a gravely ill person.

SHIR HA-SHIRIM: the Song of Songs.

SHIUR: a lesson or class on a Torah subject.

SHIVAH: the seven-day period of mourning.

SHTENDER (Y.): a lectern or bookstand.

SHTIBL(ACH) (Y.): small, intimate house(s) of prayer and study.SHUL (Y.): a synagogue.

SHULCHAN ARUCH: the authoritative Code of Jewish Law, written by Rabbi Yosef Caro in the sixteenth century.

SIFREI KODESH: holy books.

SIMCHA: a joyous occasion.

SUGYA: a specific Talmudic topic for discussion.

TALLIS: a prayer shawl worn by Jewish men.

TALMID: a student; a yeshiva student.

TALMID CHACHAM: a Torah scholar.

TANACH: the Hebrew acronym for *Torah* (Pentateuch), *Nevi'im* (Prophets), and *Kesuvim* (Hagiographa).

TEFILLAH: prayer.

TEFILLIN: two black leather boxes containing Scriptural verses, which are worn by adult males during weekday morning prayers.

TEHILLIM: [the Book of] Psalms.

TORAH, AVODAH, and GEMILUS CHASADIM: Torah observance, Divine worship, and acts of lovingkindness.

TZA'AR: sorrow.

TZADDEKES (Y.): feminine form of TZADDIK.

TZADDIK: a righteous, pious man; a holy man.

TZAROS: troubles; afflictions.

TZEDAKAH: righteousness; charity.

TZITZIS: the four-cornered fringed garment worn by males over three years of age.

TZURRES (Y., colloq.): see TZAROS.

YESHIVA: an academy of Torah study.

YICHUS: distinguished lineage.

YOM TOV: a Festival.

ZECHUS: privilege; merit.

The Sound of Soul

In a dozen different titles **Hanoch Teller** has delighted the Anglo-Jewish reader with inspiring tales of ordinary people who do extraordinary things. With a cast of fascinating characters and modern spiritual heroes and heroines, these true, contemporary stories touch the soul of readers everywhere and strike a responsive chord in their heart. Joy and drama, laughter and pathos combine to create a new genre of Jewish literature: "soul stories."

Each one of Teller's cherished tales of Jewish souls from all across the globe, skillfully written with powerful, image-evoking prose, conveys the timeless precepts of Judaism to young and old alike.

Now, in response to requests from countless educators, commuters, housewives, students, and program directors, these masterpieces have been reproduced on audio cassettes, fully dramatized with musical accompaniment and vivid sound effects.

The **Sound of Soul** volumes I & II provide over two hours of listening enjoyment for the entire family. The most heartwarming, enlightening, hilarious and poignant of Teller's tales have been transformed into an audio classic. Each cassette also contains new enchanting stories not featured in any of Hanoch Teller's books.

These high-quality tapes are not available in book stores. Please direct all orders and inquiries to:

> **Israel Media Group**
> **c/o New York City Publishing Company**
> **1 Crosswood Road**
> **Great Neck, New York 11023**